Cyril Marsters

BOY ON A BRANCH
A King's Lynn & Isle of Ely Boyhood

The Horsley Press

First published in Great Britain in 2005
by The Horsley Press
King's Lynn

ISBN 0 9524493 1 5

Printed by King's Lynn Press Ltd
Austin Fields, King's Lynn
Telephone: 01553 773011

The Horsley Press
Email: info@horsleypress.co.uk

For my children and grandchildren

Contents

BOY on a BRANCH

Part 1

Introduction

The decision to write about my life was prompted by the memory of a little childhood incident. While staying with my Grandad in his little cottage at Chapel Terrace in South Wootton, in the 1930s, I became curious about an old brass horn that hung on the wall at the top of his staircase. Though at the time the horn was being used as decoration, it must previously have been used for a purpose, I thought, and I wondered what that use might have been. When I asked Grandad about it he told me that the horn had belonged to his father – my great-grandfather – which made me even more curious. But, as is so often the case with grown-ups, it was not a convenient time for Grandad to answer further questions and I never did pursue the question any further.

In later years I have often been annoyed with myself for not probing to find out more about the old horn. Had it been a coaching horn, a hunting horn, or what? What stories had the old horn to tell; how had it come into the possession of my Great-grandad; had he used it himself, I wondered? To think that just a few more questions and answers could have given me information about my 'roots'. Old church and public records are interesting, but some first-hand information about one's great-grandparent would have been far better. Alas, the years went by, Grandad passed away and the history of the old horn died with him.

Since then, many similar opportunities have come and gone, without being grasped. But why let this situation continue? Will my own grand-children and great-grandchildren have similar questions and feel curious as I did, about the characters that were their forebears? Will they too wish that their grandparents had let them into some of the little secrets of their lives, back in the days of long ago? This then is the main reason for the narrative that follows though I hope, too, that the book will serve to amuse a wider readership. It may also prove of interest as a cameo of our working-class lives in the 1930s and '40s.

Part 1. Covers the period 1928 – 1939, the first eleven of my childhood years, in King's Lynn where I was born. During most of this time my father, Len Marsters, was a railway carriage-cleaner. Later Dad became a porter at the station and eventually, in the early spring of 1940, he obtained promotion and the family moved from Lynn to live in the station house at the little country railway station of Wilburton, in the Isle of Ely.

Part 2. Covers 1940 - 1943, the period of our stay at Wilburton station. The four years of our living there were destined to give me plenty of new experiences, some of them most enjoyable, some not so; but altogether providing a great deal of excitement. It was during this time that I reached the age of fourteen, left school and started work myself on the railway at Ely North Junction signal-box. Obviously, then, Part 2. has a strong railway flavour. On looking back, it is interesting to reflect that if my Dad's occupation had been a different one during my early years, none of these particular experiences would have come my way. It was the simple fact of his being a railwayman that was the prime cause of the whole chain of events.

CHAPTER 1

Beginnings and Early Life in King's Lynn

I was born at number 16 Kirby Street, a small terraced house, in the market town of King's Lynn, on May 14th 1928. My brother Geoff arrived a year later in May 1929 and my sister in the January of 1931 – all at the same address. Our birth certificates state that at the time when we arrived, Dad was a Railway Carriage Cleaner. He worked for the London & North Eastern Railway Company at the railway station in Blackfriars Road, barely five minutes walk from our house. Sometime later, before the family eventually left Lynn, he changed jobs and became a porter at the station, but for the first eight or nine years of my life he was a carriage cleaner.

Kirby Street ran between Norfolk Street at its top (northern) end and Wellesley Street at the other end. The two rows of terraced houses occupied only the top half of the street. On one side of the bottom half, behind a wooden close-boarded fence, was a rough scrubby area of land. The local children used to call this the 'wood-yard' and we often used to play there. We used to gain access where a few of the fence boards were conveniently missing. On the other side of the road was an enclosed yard belonging to Hallack & Bond the grocery wholesalers. Their adjacent warehouse stood on the Kirby street corner at the junction with Wellesley Street.

Exactly how long we lived in No.16 Kirby Street, I'm not sure. Whilst we were still quite young, some neighbours – Mr and Mrs Walker and their son Lenny - moved out of number 14, the house next-door-but-one. For some reason I'm not aware of, my parents obtained the tenancy of the vacant house and moved the short distance along the street. As far as I can remember the houses were of virtually identical layout; the only reason for the move which I can imagine was that the 'new' house had the benefit of rather more outhouse space in the back yard. No. 14 was to remain our home until shortly before the War began in 1939.

Most houses in the street, like our own, were 'two-up, two-downers', though a few of them had a scullery extension at the rear. Our small kitchen was at the back of the house, and the slightly bigger living room at the front, the latter always being referred to as the 'front room'. The front door in this room led straight to the street outside. The narrow staircase leading up to the front bedroom was gained through a door at the side of the front room. One had to go through the front bedroom to reach the back one. Our parents used the front bedroom; my brother Geoff and I shared a double bed in the back one. Our younger sister's cot occupied a corner in our parent's room. The rent, I think, was seven shillings per week and sometimes on a Saturday morning I would be given the errand of taking the payment along to Langford & Fidment's tobacconist's shop in Blackfriars Road. Presumably the proprietors of the shop were also the landlords of our house. I well remember the characteristic smells of the various tobaccos on sale in the shop.

The house was supplied with mains electricity, but only for lighting which consisted of a single light bulb in the centre of the ceiling in each room. Payment for the electricity was made by putting shillings in a meter, located on the wall in the front room. There were no modern power points in the house in those days. Current for running our 'wireless' set was supplied by an 'accumulator'. This was a re-chargeable electric cell, contained in a glass outer case and with a carrying handle at the top. We had two of these: one in use on the set and the other would be up at Curry's shop in the High street for re-charging. The current would last about a week, when the discharged accumulator would be taken to the shop and the fresh one collected. Whenever I was sent on this errand, I remember, I was told to be careful not to spill any of the acid. The re-charging cost each time was sixpence.

There was no public access behind the house, the concrete back yard being surrounded by a wall. In a corner of the yard furthest from the house was a brick-built 'flush' lavatory. Opposite this was some shedding, split into two sections. Dad used the far section for storing tools, brooms, etc. The other shed section had an open end facing the back of the house and contained the items needed by Mum for doing the weekly wash.

These included the copper in which the water was heated and the big mangle, used for squeezing out the water from the washed clothes and bed linen. Also stored in the shed was our tin bath, which used to hang on a nail on the wall.

The copper was a big metal basin-shaped receptacle, built into a square brick structure of about three feet in height, with the round open top of the copper flush with the top of the bricks. A round removable wooden lid, with a handle on top, fitted above the top rim of the copper. When hot water was required a small fireplace, built into the brickwork beneath, heated the water in the copper, which had a capacity of about 10 gallons.

The mangle had two big wooden rollers, one above the other, fitted into a cast-iron frame. These were turned by hand by means of a large wheel with a protruding handle at the right-hand end of the rollers. Wet clothes, after being washed and before putting them on the line to dry, had most of the water squeezed out by neatly folding them and then passing them between the rollers. This was quite an energetic job; sometimes I would help by turning the handle, while Mum would insert the folded clothes between the front of the rollers and deftly retrieve them from behind. When she was alone and had to turn the handle herself, the clothes were allowed to drop onto a shelf at the back of the mangle, as you could not reach round to collect them until you had let go of the handle.

The portable galvanised 'tin bath' would be brought in from the shed into the kitchen every Friday evening for each of us to use in turn for our regular weekly bath. As was done for the clothes wash, the water needed for bathing would also be heated in the outside copper. When hot, it was carried inside in buckets for filling the bath.

The metal dustbin used for household rubbish, fire-ash, etc. was kept in the backyard. Once a week this had to be carried through the house to the street outside, for collection by the refuse cart – or the dustcart, as we used to call it; the operators were known as dustmen. The yard itself was kept clean by Dad. After swilling it down with buckets of water containing Jeyes fluid disinfectant, he would energetically sweep the concrete, directing the water towards the drain in the corner of the yard

Today, in 2005, none of the little terraced houses of Kirby Street remain. They were demolished, in the early 1970s I believe, and were replaced by a development of grouped homes for the elderly, named Emmerich Court. However, recently I was surprised to discover that the Kirby Street name boards are still in place at both ends of the old street.

Carriage Cleaning

Dad's carriage cleaning job involved a 4.30 am start every day – what today we would call 'un-social hours', or as my Grandad used to describe it: "Going out before the streets were aired." This early start meant that Dad had to get out of bed at about 4 am and to ensure that he awoke on time he used to wind up his big metal alarm clock every night on going to bed. The clock had two bells on top with a striking hammer that made quite a loud noise. In order not to waken the family he used to place the clock beneath his pillows to muffle the sound of the alarm. When it went off he would slide his hand under the pillow to turn it off.

After getting up and having a cup of tea, Dad would take his bag containing the sandwiches, which had been packed up the night before and, noiselessly leaving the house, he would walk the short distance to the station in Blackfriars road. I used to think how silly it seemed that the road running past the station was called Blackfriars, but the parallel road actually called Railway Road was a whole block away and did not pass the station at all. I expect that there was some historical reason for this but I never did find out what it was.

Dad would finish work at about 1 p.m. each day and, as we children used to have quite a long midday break from school in those days, one or other of us would often wait at the end of our street to meet him when he left off. I would see him turn the corner into Wellesley street, in his blue overall trousers and jacket, plus his railway cap, and he could very well have been mistaken for an engine driver and I used to imagine him in that rather more glamorous job. The fact that he arrived home every day just a few minutes past 1 p.m. and we didn't have to be back at school until 2 o'clock, meant that the whole family were able to sit down to our mid-day dinner together as a regular routine.

Early Schooling

The first school I attended, immediately after my fifth birthday, was 'Highgate Infants' school on the Gaywood road. On my first day I was taken to school by Dad on his bicycle. The bike had a child's seat on the cross-bar, with some little metal stirrups hanging on leather straps, for my feet. On one occasion when riding on this seat I managed to get a foot caught in the spokes of the wheel, which caused both Dad and me to be thrown forward over the handlebars, which didn't please him! I remember being quite indignant, on the day he took me to school, that I had to start school so soon after my birthday. I thought that I should have been allowed time to get used to the idea first. In reality, I suppose that I was feeling quite apprehensive as to what to expect.

I need not have worried: the lady teacher seemed to go out of her way to impress upon me that school was not a daunting experience at all. All I remember about that first day was: a.) being given some empty match boxes and shown how to do some modelling with them and b.) the milk we had at break time. We had to take a half-penny to pay for the milk, which was contained in little bottles of one-third of a pint each. The bottles had cardboard tops with a little perforated circle in the middle that was pushed out so that the drinking straw could be inserted.

In those days, these drinking straws were actually made from genuine straw. I don't remember what happened in the admission class, but later on in the higher classes, when it was milk time, the box containing the straws would be taken round the class by one of the children, the 'straw monitor', for each child to take one. As the straws were a natural product, not a synthetic one as they are today, their internal diameters used to vary. For some reason the fat ones were the ones we all used to covet and so they were the ones which were selected first, leaving the thin ones for those who were unlucky enough to be handed the box later.

Of the lessons, the one I remember best is the English lesson: learning the letters of the alphabet phonetically - getting used to their different sounds and then learning how they went together to form words. I used to quite enjoy those lessons and picked things up quite quickly. Another lesson that sticks in the memory and which was obviously intended to encourage creativity, was when we were given the materials to make up some dough for making miniature loaves, pastries and cakes, sweets etc. We would then paint them and set them out, like a display in a baker's or a confectioners window; plenty of scope for individual imagination.

Of my fellow pupils, I only remember one name, a boy named Horace Rocket who used to sit immediately in front of me. 'Horry', as we used to call him, had red hair, but his distinguishing feature that struck me most, was the pronounced circular pattern of the hair on the crown of his head. It always reminded me of the spinning 'Catherine wheel' fireworks we sometimes had on Guy Fawkes night and which Dad would pin on an upright post before lighting them. It was fortunate that I never had a pin handy when I sat behind Horry, for I'm sure that I would have been tempted to stick it through the centre of the very distinct crown at the back of his head.

My next school was St. James Boys Junior school, just off the London Road, and my time there was also quite happy and enjoyable. Apart from the basic tuition of the 'three Rs', at which I was fairly competent, I used to look forward to Friday afternoons, the last period of which was usually an Art lesson. 'Art' was rather a loose term for a free and easy session of drawing and painting something of our own choice - I don't remember any formal teaching of drawing or painting techniques. For quite a number of weeks my drawing was almost always of an ocean liner, until the teacher, noticing my 'one-track' mind told me I was being unimaginative and persuaded me to try different subjects.

Our Headmaster was Mr Scales, a very apt name I thought, for once a week he would take our class of about thirty-five boys for a 'singing' session. 'Old Skilly' – as we boys had irreverently nicknamed him – taught us some rousing songs, such as: 'While We were Marching through

Georgia', 'Hearts of Oak are our Ships' and many others, which we would sing with gusto. Usually, when he was teaching us a new song, he would give us a little information on its historical background; one such song went as follows:

South Caroline is a sultry clime
Where we used to work in the summer time.
Massa neath de shade would lay
While we poor darkies toiled all day *(sic)*

Chorus:
So early in de mornin', so early in de mornin',
So early in de mornin', before de break of day.

When I was young and used to wait
On Massa's table, lay de plate,
Pass de bottle when him dry,
Brush away de blue-tail fly.

Chorus: …

Now Massa 's dead and gone to rest,
Of all de Massas he was best,
Never seen de like since ah was born,
Miss him now he's dead and gone.

Chorus:…

To sing a song like this in school today would be regarded as racist, but Skilly used the opportunity to teach us about the evils of slavery which had taken place in earlier years in the American plantations and elsewhere.

These singing lessons took place in the school hall with the boys standing in rows in the body of the hall. Skilly, when he was not at the piano teaching us the tune of a new song, would stand on the raised

7

platform. From here he would take us through our repertoire, keeping us in time by conducting us with a heavy old-fashioned cylindrical ruler as a baton.

The weight of this 'baton' must have provided quite a bit of exercise for Skilly's right arm, but that didn't concern us - there was another rather disconcerting use to which he occasionally put this instrument. We would be in full voice with a song, when he would come down from the platform, walk up and down behind the rows and, with his hand cupped round his ear he would listen closely to each boy's singing. Then, if he thought it necessary, he would tap a boy smartly on the head with the baton and say: "You're flat, boy" - or whatever criticism he thought appropriate. Luckily I managed to miss any of these cracks on the head and, apart from having to be alert for this unnerving habit of 'Skilly's', I much enjoyed his singing lessons.

Grandad
Our paternal grandfather, Henry George Marsters, was the only grandparent that Geoff, Joan and I had ever known during our 1930s childhood. Grandma, his wife, had died of meningitis at the early age of forty-five, before we were born. Mum's parents, the Horsleys, were also dead and so we had no memory of them either. This must have been one of the reasons why 'Grandad' meant so much to us – we were extremely fond of him and, as we knew, so he was of us.

Dad was a short man, but Grandad was even smaller, barely five feet tall. But what he lacked in stature he made up for in other ways – he was quite a character. One distinctive feature was his large moustache. This reminds me of a little habit of his which used to amuse us children but greatly annoyed Mum. If his tea was too hot he would tip some into the saucer and drink from that, making his long moustache all wet in the process. Geoff and I used to privately joke that Grandad used his moustache to filter the tealeaves from his tea.

Whilst Grandma had been alive, and when their two sons had been growing up, the family had lived at No.3 Lodge Cottages, Manor Road in North Wootton. Grandad was employed as a groom-gardener by Mr. Blomfield of Manor farm, at the end of the road. Later, when his sons had grown up, he changed to farm work and moved to No.1 Chapel Terrace, at South Wootton. Here, he still worked for Mr. Blomfield who had farms at both North and South Wootton. This little Chapel Terrace cottage, where he lived alone, was Grandad's home that we were familiar with as children.

Though Grandad lived on his own during the week, he came to us for dinner and tea on most weekends. Chapel Terrace was only about two-and-a-half miles from Kirby Street and he would either cycle over to us, or come on one of the frequent Eastern Counties buses that ran between Lynn and South Wootton. He would sometimes bring with him one of his favourite delicacies to share with us at tea time, either a brawn pie or a pint of cockles.

Whilst on the subject of food, another notable feature about Grandad was the way he chewed his meals; he had no teeth. We kids accepted this without question for we had never known him with any teeth; in any case Grandad was a law unto himself, as we instinctively knew. According to Mother he had once been fitted up with a set of false teeth but, after trying them for the first time, had discarded them in disgust. Ever since then he had relied on his gums for mastication and by now they seemed to be able to tackle almost anything.

A cheerful, straightforward little man, Grandad's pleasures in life were simple. He loved a brisk walk to observe what was going on around and about the town and he would often take me with him. The first requirement before setting off was to stoke up his beloved pipe, an article that he never seemed to be without. Pulling his favourite 'Digger Mixture' tobacco from his tobacco pouch, he would carefully tamp it down bit by bit into the bowl of the pipe, then light up from his box of 'Swan Vestas' matches. After he had given a few hard draws on the pipe to get it going well, we would set off. The walking stick in his right hand would go 'stump, stump' in time with his left foot; occasionally it would come up with a flourish in front of him, then drop down again on the second beat, so to speak.

Over a period Grandad and I must have walked many miles. One walk I much enjoyed was along the cockle-shell roadway down past the Fisher Fleet. There used to be one or two abandoned old wrecks of boats along the banks and which I could briefly explore as we passed. The Ferry, which plied backwards and forwards over the river, was another excitement. I had never previously been on this, as the family normally had no cause to use it. However, Grandad provided this new experience for me: he took me down the narrow Ferry Lane to the landing stage and across the river on the little boat to see a friend of his at West Lynn.

Another of my favourite places to visit was the South Quay, alongside the river. There would very often be a ship berthed there that we could watch being loaded or unloaded. Much of the freight in those days was taken to and from the ships by rail; there was a railway track along the length of the quay and over the two swing bridges. One of these bridges crossed the Millfleet and the other the nearby river Nar.

I never saw any actual locomotives along the quay – I think they were too heavy to be allowed over the bridges. The shunting of the wagons was carried out by agricultural-type tractors. These tractors had big metal plates fitted across their fronts and rears, at the same height as the railway vehicle buffers, so that they could push the trucks along. In addition to the tractors, capstans and cables were also used at certain points, I think. It was normal in those days for people to use the quay-side and the swing bridges as part of a riverside walk. However, I don't think that the bridges were intended to accommodate railway wagons and pedestrians at one and the same time – you had to look out for any shunting operations before starting to cross.

Grandad sometimes would take me with him when he visited his other relations who lived in Lynn: his sister Matilda Snare and his brother James Marsters. Aunt Till, as his sister was known in the family, was a widow living in South Street. I recall sitting in her front room, conscious of a background of the low hiss of a lighted gas-lamp on a wall, and the leisurely tick of her pendulum clock, as she and Grandad busily chatted together. They always seemed to have plenty of news to catch up on and would talk for ages. Aunt Till used to attend the nearby St Johns church and I remember her telling Grandad about a previous Sunday's sermon and how nice a man the Vicar was. After a while I would only be half listening to them: the chatter, plus the hiss of the lamp and the measured tick of the clock was so relaxing that I would go off into a reverie of my own until it was time to leave again.

Uncle Jim, as Grandad's brother James was known, lived with his wife Anna in a small cottage somewhere in North Lynn. The exact whereabouts escapes me – all I remember is of approaching the door through the tiniest of gardens, which held a bright display of fragrant Pinks. My main preoccupation here, whist the grown-ups chatted, was in studying the brown biscuit barrel standing on the sideboard and which, I knew, contained ginger biscuits. They were not any old ginger biscuits, like the hard ones we sometimes had at home, but were moist and chewy – just as I liked them. Usually my patience would be rewarded; on seeing my longing look at the barrel, Aunt Anna would take off the lid and offer me some.

One of the couple would be bound to remark as to how much I had grown since they had last seen me. Grandad's response was always the same; he would say: 'Yes, at the rate he is growing I think he will have to be a policeman when he grows up.' This however was rather over-optimistic on Grandad's part, for though I eventually attained a height of about five feet eight inches – taller than anyone of my immediate family – this was not enough for the police force. The minimum height allowed for becoming a police constable in those days was six feet.

While out and about with Grandad, especially during the summer, I would keep a lookout in the hope of seeing an ice-cream man. These men used to pedal around on purpose-built tricycles that had a large insulated box, containing the ice cream, between the two front wheels. A lid on the top gave access to the contents. Painted in big letters on the front of the box was the invitation to: STOP ME AND BUY ONE. The rider's seat was on the frame behind the box and his pedals drove the single back wheel. A handle across the back of the box, plus a hinge in the frame, allowed the tricycle to be steered by turning the whole box and the front wheels. The weight of this machine must have made hard work of both pedalling and steering it.

This last thought never used to occur to me as a child, of course; I was only interested in the products in the box. Grandad would always come up trumps when we met one of these vehicles and would delve into his trouser pocket and find me a penny. About the cheapest item on sale, which I liked and would usually buy, was a kind of iced lolly that came in various colours and flavours. It was about six inches in length, of triangular section and, instead of being on a stick, was contained in a thin cardboard sleeve. You pushed the ice up through the sleeve and sucked it from the end. I think that there were various ice cream companies who used to use these tricycles: Walls, I think was one of them and the other one I remember was El Dorado.

Sometimes during our walks Grandad would meet an acquaintance of his and this would entail a stop and a 'mardle' – sometimes a lengthy one. At the start I would listen to their conversations with interest, but gradually becoming bored I would begin to wish they would stop talking so that we could get on our way again. But I knew that I had to wait for the point – which always came eventually – when Grandad would draw the conversation to a close with the words: 'Ah well t'gither, I shull hatta be a drawin on now, dew I shan't git round.'

Grandad's Puttees. One winter's afternoon Grandad arrived at ours for tea, having cycled straight from work. He was wearing something on his lower legs that I had never seen him in before and he reminded me of the pictures I had seen of soldiers in the trenches during the 1914-18 war. Being very curious about these items of attire, which made a neat regular pattern round his legs from just above his boots and nearly up to his knees, I asked him what they were. He told me that they were puttees.

He said that he had been working that day with a threshing gang and when the bottom of the stack was reached there were a lot of rats to deal with. An area round the stack had been enclosed with stakes and netting to stop the escape of the rats so that they could be caught and killed. This prevented them doing damage elsewhere. Grandad had worn the puttees to protect his legs, he told me. This set my imagination working – I could see Grandad, without any puttees on and surrounded by rats, which were all trying to get inside the legs of his trousers to hide. A nasty thought! Yes, puttees definitely seemed a good idea.

Grandad sat down on a kitchen chair to take the puttees off, whilst I looked on to see the mystery revealed. They were long strips of cloth that had been neatly and evenly wound spirally round and round the legs. I couldn't understand how they had stayed in place all day without becoming unwound or out of place, but they obviously had. Just how the ends were secured – whether they were simply tucked in, or fixed by safety pins – I cannot now recall. Having taken them off Grandad rolled them up and put them in his haversack.

One too many?

The following little anecdote concerning Grandad is not a boyhood memory of mine, but a little tale laughingly told me by my mother much later in life. I thought that she must have been exaggerating a little, but she assured me that it was true. One day, during the period when she and Dad were courting, they had been for a walk round the Woottons. When they were on their way back to Dad's home at Chapel Terrace, they became aware of a cyclist catching them up from behind and who was obviously under the influence of a few pints. Unable to ride straight he was veering from one side of the road to the other.

They thought that they recognised the outline of the approaching figure and, as he got nearer their suspicions were confirmed − it was Dad's father. Thinking that they ought to take charge and help him home, they stood and waited for him to come alongside. However, as he drew level he showed not the slightest sign of recognition and continued pedalling furiously along the road − still weaving badly from side to side. The courting couple hurried along fearful that before they got to the cottage they would find 'Grandad' in a heap on the road. On arriving home shortly after, they found Grandad upstairs, fast asleep on his bed − still with his boots on!

Very obviously, in those days Grandad had been partial to his pint, But I think that this little episode must have been a rather exceptional one, rather than a regular habit. If not, then he was certainly a reformed character later, for in my young days I never knew him to touch alcohol at all.

CHAPTER 2

A Visit to Chapel Terrace

Although we used to see quite a lot of Grandad at Kirby Street, we would also visit him occasionally in his own cottage at South Wootton. One visit, in particular, remains vividly in my mind. I would have been quite young – about eight I think – and it was the first time that I went alone to see Grandad. It was also the first time that I had been allowed to travel on the bus on my own, so the occasion was something of a milestone in my young life.

The visit had obviously been pre-arranged, for Mum informed me on the Saturday morning that I was to stay overnight at Grandad's and then return home on the bus with him the next morning. At the time, Grandad was recovering from a bout of influenza and so he had not done any recent shopping. Mum had therefore packed a basket with a few groceries for him, which I was to take with me. In spite of having one of my favourite foods for breakfast that morning – bread and dripping – Mum had to insist on me finishing my breakfast, for with the excitement of the prospect of my 'grown-up' unescorted journey, I was anxious to get started.

When at last I was ready, I walked the short distance from Kirby Street round to the bus stop at 'Townsend's Corner', as it was known. This was a corner at the junction of Railway Road and Norfolk Street. A shop on the site was occupied by Charles Townsend Limited, the corn and seed merchants – hence the name by which the bus-stop just outside the shop was known. It was from this shop a few years later that I came to buy food for a pair of pet mice I was given.

In the 1930s Norfolk Street, at this point, formed the top of a 'T' junction at the end of Railway Road (not yet then having been opened up for access to the later John Kennedy Road). All through traffic at the time had to pass through the town. Traffic going north travelled along London Road, St. James' Road and Railway Road, then turned right into Norfolk Street at this 'T' junction and continued on through Gaywood. Southbound traffic used the same route in the reverse direction.

The buses that ran between the Millfleet bus station and South Wootton were quite frequent and I had not long to wait at the bus stop. I felt very grown-up as I boarded the bus, told the conductor my destination and handed him my fare – a penny, I think it was. The distance of the short journey being only slightly over a couple of miles, it was not very long before I got off the bus again, at the little green at the South Wootton cross-roads. The buses used to turn round this green and wait there for a few minutes before returning to Lynn. Of the roads radiating from this junction, I knew that I was to ignore the Grimston and the Castle Rising roads and take the other one which led further down into the village – Low Road, I think it was called.

As I walked down this road looking at the various houses I passed, one dwelling in particular much intrigued me. This was an old railway carriage, which had been converted for use as a home – which seemed to me a brilliant idea. It must be exciting to live in such an unusual home, I thought. Strangely enough, on passing this same spot nearly seventy years later in the summer of 2004, I was amazed to see the same property, still performing sterling service as a home. Today, of course, such enterprising initiative for creating a home would not be allowed by the planning authorities.

After passing two roads that went off to the right, Nursery Lane and Hall Lane, I soon reached Chapel Terrace on the left-hand side. Grandad's cottage was the very first one you came to. The hard road had narrowed here and, if my memory is correct, it was not much more than a lane where it passed along the fences of the small front gardens. This was certainly the case where it continued on past the last building, a small Methodist chapel that stood alone just beyond the last cottage. Here the roadway was no more than a farm track, leading to the fields beyond the chapel.

The Lane beyond the Chapel. Author.

The contrast between this spot and our street in Lynn was tremendous, and I loved it. The outlook in Kirby Street was restricted by a dull row of terraced houses on both sides of the street. Here at Wootton, from the front of Grandad's cottage, the view was of fields, hedges and vegetation. Also, there was something mysterious about the way in which the little roadway, reduced to a green track after passing the chapel, disappeared into the fields and the 'secret unknown' beyond. I'm sure that for both Geoff and me in the 1930s, the character of this place epitomised the very essence of 'country' as opposed to town.

This happy impression of Grandad's home and surroundings was to remain embedded in my memory. Much later, on returning to Norfolk after many years' absence, and yielding to the urge to visit old haunts, I came again to view Chapel Terrace. The short terrace with its little cottages, plus the chapel at the end, are indeed still there – in fact, looking hardly changed since I was a boy. But there the likeness ends; time and 'progress' have intervened to destroy the boyhood magic.

The illusion of that mysterious hinterland, to which the green lane had once beckoned, has been broken. Now, one is simply led back into Lynn on a new and busy by-pass – the Edward Benefer Way. I cannot imagine that the residents of Chapel Terrace were ecstatic at its coming, or at the creation of the industrial and commercial estates that have sprung up alongside it. Fortunately for them, the by-pass has not actually taken over the little roadway immediately in front of the dwellings, but has been sited a few yards further away. Nevertheless the heavy traffic passes by parallel to, and a short distance from their front gardens, shattering the peace and removing the open views of previous years. But then, we cannot impede progress, I suppose.

As I reached Grandad's front gate and entered his garden, he spotted me from the window. I had barely opened the porch door and stepped inside before he had the inner door open and was beckoning me into the house. We greeted each other and, remembering that he had just got over the 'flu, I asked how he was feeling. He said that he was much better now, but fed up with being indoors and impatient to get out into the fresh air. He took my coat from me, asked me to sit down and said that he would make a pot of tea.

There were a number of differences between Grandad's cottage and our house in Lynn and also differences in the way he lived. To me, there was a certain indefinable aura about his home which made it peculiarly 'Grandad'; a quite strong childhood impression, I remember. Whether this feeling was simply the result of all the little differences that I had become aware of – or something more – I don't know.

The first difference you noticed was on entering his front porch, for this had a characteristic odour of paraffin oil. The spaces underneath two built-in seats in the porch were used for storage, part of which was used to house Grandad's paraffin containers. Unlike us, he had no electricity and relied on oil-lamps to provide his lighting; hence the need for the containers for his spare oil supply. The porch itself was another difference, of course. To have a porch seemed a good idea; not only to use as storage space bur also, as Grandad pointed out, to stop cold drafts coming straight into the house when the front door was opened. It would not have been possible for us to have a porch in Kirby Street, for our front room door opened directly onto the public pavement in the street outside.

Grandad's cottage was similar to our house in that they both had only four rooms – two downstairs and two bedrooms – but the ground floor ones were the opposite way round. His kitchen was at the front and the parlour at the back. I have no doubt that when Grandma had been alive the parlour would have been in use, but during my childhood Grandad never seemed to enter it. He used the other room as both kitchen and living room. His table was positioned near the front window so, whilst sitting in his wheel-back chair at the table he could see out into the front garden and observe the comings and goings in the lane beyond. A small black range, with its little fire-grate and side oven, in the chimney at one end of the kitchen gave the room a very cosy feel. On the wall at the side of the range hung a copper warming pan and, as I was to learn at bedtime on that particular day, this implement was not hanging on the wall simply as decoration.

Grandad chatted to me as we sat and drank our tea. When we had finished it he said: 'It's time I stretched my legs; we will take a walk up to the blacksmiths – I've some tools that need sharpening.' From the outhouse at the back of the cottage, he fetched a billhook and a slasher. This rather puzzled me for I had previously seen him sharpen such tools himself, using a rub-stone. On asking him about it he told me that they needed some extra grinding down on the blacksmith's big grindstone. He put the tools into a hessian sack, tied this round with a piece of string and we set off up the road towards the junction where earlier I had arrived on the bus.

As we passed by the converted railway-carriage I remarked to Grandad that this was an unusual sort of home to live in. I wondered whether it was the type of carriage where all the compartments were separate – which was what it looked like – or whether it was a coach with a corridor. It would be very inconvenient, I thought, if it had no corridor, as you would then have to go outside and come back in again every time you wished to move between one room and another. Grandad pointed out that the owners had built an extension onto the back of the coach, which had solved the problem.

When we reached the green we turned towards Lynn and passed by the New Inn on our right-hand side. Beyond this stood Blake's cycle shop and, a bit further back from the road, was the blacksmith's shop itself, also run by the Blakes, I later discovered. I was disappointed to find that there were no horses in the smithy when we arrived, for I had been hoping to see one shod. Grandad and the blacksmith seemed to have lots to mardle about, so whilst they were chatting I amused myself by looking round the smithy at the various tools and materials around the place. Eventually the conversation came to an end and, with Grandad turning the handle, the blacksmith sharpened the tools on his big grinding wheel. Grandad bade the blacksmith farewell and we retraced our steps to Chapel Terrace.

Our morning excursion had given me an appetite, so on arrival back at the cottage I was pleased to hear Grandad say: 'Time to be getting dinner ready, t'gither'. He asked me to bring in some potatoes from a sack in the outhouse whilst he went to cut a cabbage in the back garden. After preparing the vegetables Grandad looked in Mum's grocery basket and found a tin of baked beans. The label on the tin stated that as well as beans it also contained pork pieces. They would 'go down well' with the potatoes and greens, he decided, and he opened the tin and tipped the contents into a small saucepan. On taking a closer look into the saucepan he remarked: 'whoever put the pork pieces in must have thrown them in from a distance − and their aim wasn't very good!' In spite of the paucity of the meat content I thoroughly enjoyed our meal. Neither was I disappointed at the lack of a pudding, for I knew that Grandad's cooking was rather basic and I had not expected any.

Later, after we had done justice to a pot of tea, Grandad asked what I would like to do during the afternoon. He knew that I was keen on drawing and, taking a short pencil from his waistcoat pocket, he offered to find me a piece of paper so that I could draw. However, on this occasion I had other ideas. When I had fetched the potatoes in for dinner I had spotted some of Grandad's tools in the outhouse and thought that it would be fun to use some carpentry tools − something I had not yet had chance to try. Declining his proffered 'piece of cedar' (Grandad's name for a pencil), I asked him instead whether I could borrow some tools and go outside to make a model ship.

Taking me round to the outhouse, Grandad handed me a hammer, a saw and an old tobacco tin containing a collection of nails. After a search he found some bits of wood which I thought would be suitable for my model and finally, gave me an old stool for cutting the wood on. Then, after warning me to be careful not to cut myself with the saw, he went indoors to read his newspaper. Unlike my earlier quick visit for potatoes, I now had chance to look round the outhouse contents in more detail. As with the cottage, the shed seemed to have taken on a personality of its own − typical 'Grandad'. His bicycle was propped on one side and on the walls hung all his gardening tools, plus various others such as the hedging tools that we had taken to the blacksmith's that morning for sharpening. There were all sorts of other things: rabbit snares, mole traps and some things which I had never seen before. One of the items in particular I couldn't begin to guess the purpose of.

This tool was made up of a six-inch length of metal that was bent length-wise into a rounded sort of tunnel shape, the bottom edges of which were serrated with small teeth. A wooden handle was fixed at a right angle to the top of the tool. When I enquired about it later, Grandad told me that it was called a curry comb and was used for grooming horses. I suppose that the tool was a memento from his earlier days as a groom at North Wootton. Little did I imagine when asking Grandad about it, that as time went by I would myself handle such a tool very frequently on a Cambridgeshire farm, to groom Percheron heavy horses. But that day was some time yet in the future.

Coming back to the day in question: after snapping out of the reverie caused by thinking about Grandad's tools, I remembered that I had been intending to make a model ship. I sorted out a length of wood suitable for the hull, tapered one end of this with two cuts of the saw to form the prow and then, with a number of smaller cuts the other end, made a roughly rounded stern. The raised sections of the forecastle, the bridge and the stern, I made by nailing shorter pieces of wood on top of the hull. Then, after nailing through from underneath, I managed to attach a very clumsy looking funnel. The result, I thought, was a recognisable model of a tramp steamer, similar to ones I had seen moored at the South Quay in Lynn.

Though my model must have been very crude, I was quite proud of my creation and I took it indoors for Grandad to admire – which he duly did. When he had made the appropriate comments about the boat, he asked me to put his tools away and to shut the outhouse door, as it would soon be tea-time. I did as he asked and as I did so I realised how chilly it had become outside, something I had not been aware of whilst concentrating on my 'boat-building'. On coming back indoors it was very nice to sit and warm myself in front of the cosy kitchen range. Tea that night, I seem to remember, was a simple meal of bread, butter and jam. There was none of the cockles or other sea-food which I knew Grandad was partial to; however, there was plenty of bread to fill up with and, of course, the essential pot of tea.

By the time we had finished tea and the crockery had been cleared away, the daylight coming through the window had faded and the room had become quite dim. At home in the evenings we would simply switch on a light, but here there was no electricity in the cottage. I always found it absorbing, therefore, to watch as Grandad lit his oil-lamp. Placing the lamp in the middle of the table he took off the glass globe, lit the wick with a match and then replaced the globe. The wick had to be adjusted, up or down, by means of a little knob, until the flame was burning brightly and without any smoke and during this process it emitted its characteristic odour, which was all part of the novelty for me. Eventually, when the lamp was burning properly, the smell given off by the paraffin-soaked wick would diminish until it was no longer noticeable. The light from the lamp somehow seemed much softer and friendlier than the harsh light of an electric bulb.

When the lamp was burning to his satisfaction Grandad found me a piece of paper, took out the little 'piece of cedar' from his waistcoat pocket, and I was able to sit at the table and amuse myself by drawing until bedtime. Grandad himself settled back into his wheel-back chair to read his Lynn newspaper – the 'Advertiser' as he always called it. The Lynn Advertiser, as I recall seeing Grandad reading it, was a large newspaper of the broadsheet type – as also was, I believe, its rival paper the Lynn News. I have since learned that in 1944 under the pressure of wartime restrictions, the two papers merged to form the Lynn News & Advertiser. In 1989 the paper converted to tabloid format and shortened its title to the Lynn News, as it is still published today.

Later that evening when Grandad decided that it was time for me to get ready for bed, he poured some warm water into a bowl, from the kettle on the range, for me to have a wash. As I dutifully carried out this routine, he took down from the wall beside the chimney that novel piece of hardware – the big copper warming pan, which I had never seen in use before. As I watched, he opened the lid of the pan and then, holding a folded cloth, he took a couple of bricks that he had been heating on the kitchen range, put them inside and closed the lid again. Saying that he would warm the bed up for me before I went up, he disappeared up the stairs. On chilly nights at home we used to warm the beds with stoneware hot-water-bottles; a warming pan was indeed a novelty to me, but apparently quite normal here at Chapel Terrace.

A little later Grandad accompanied me upstairs, the warming pan was transferred to his side of the bed and I was tucked in on the warmed side. The bed felt luxurious; you sank down into the soft feather mattress that seemed to form a kind of nest around you and, together with the nicely warmed area at your feet, gave a sense of blissful comfort. This was quite a contrast to the much harder flock mattress that I shared with my brother Geoff at home. It could not have been very long before I dropped off to sleep and I didn't hear Grandad when he came up to bed.

When I awoke next morning the curtains were still drawn across the bedroom window, but I could see that it was broad daylight outside. Grandad had already gone downstairs. Jumping out of bed and pulling back the curtains, I looked out onto the lane below and a cold but bright, fine morning. Pouring a little cold water from the flower patterned jug into the matching basin on the washstand I gave my face a token rub to wash the sleep from my eyes and started to dress. I observed that, apart from the bed with its iron frame, and the washstand, the rest of the furniture in the room consisted of a couple of small bedroom chairs and a dressing table with a mirror on top.

On one end of the dressing table lay a small bible, which made me wonder, for as far as I knew Grandad never attended church, or was religiously inclined. The bible, some small ornaments and the dressing table itself, I noticed, were all covered in a thin layer of dust. I noticed too that on the floor, and especially under the bed, were numerous small feathers that had obviously escaped from the feather bed, or the pillows. This was quite a contrast with home, for Mum was very particular to keep everything dusted and clean.

On going downstairs into the kitchen I found Grandad preparing for breakfast. I asked him about the little bible I'd seen upstairs. He replied: 'That belonged to your Grandmother'. I also told him that his bedroom was dusty and that the feathers needed clearing up from under his bed and offered to have a tidy-up for him. He agreed that this would be a good idea, but said to leave it until after breakfast. Grandad had earlier got the fire going in the kitchen range and now had a saucepan of water on for boiling eggs for breakfast. He had laid the table with plates, eggcups, cups and saucers and a plate of bread and butter. I noticed from his cup, that Grandad had already had a cup of tea whilst waiting for me to get up; the enamel teapot now stood on the side of the range next to the black kettle.

When the eggs were cooked Grandad transferred them to the eggcups and we sat down for breakfast. Again, as I sat opposite the window looking out onto the front garden, the contrast between here and home was striking – at home we had only the back concrete yard to look out at. After breakfast I reminded Grandad about the dust and feathers in his bedroom and asked him for a brush and dustpan and a duster so that I could clean them up. He got these out for me but told me not to take too long as he wanted us to catch the ten o'clock bus to Lynn, so I hurried upstairs to start the clean up. At the top of the stairs I saw a brass horn, hanging by its braided cord on the wall of the tiny landing. I had not noticed this earlier and was very curious to know what sort of horn it was: how old was it - where had it come from – what had it been used for – how had it come into Grandad's possession?

I swept up the feathers from under and around the bed. Then, moving the ornaments as I had seen Mum do at home, I dusted the top of the dressing table. The last thing I picked up was the little bible, and dusted its cover. It was a strange feeling: I was handling a possession of *my* Grandma's – but a Grandma I had never seen. Dad had once told me that his mother had died quite young, of meningitis. Turning over a few pages of the bible I went into a reverie, wondering what she had been like. Being so fond of Grandad, I was sure that we would have loved her too and I felt sad that she had died before I was born and I had never had chance to get to know her.

A call from downstairs reminded me that we were to catch the ten o'clock bus, so I hurried down. Remembering the brass horn that hung on the landing, I asked Grandad about it. He said that it had belonged to his father – my great-grandfather. This, of course, excited further questions from me. But Grandad was now impatient for me to get ready and to start walking to get the bus, so I dismissed the questions from my mind and did as I was told.

CHAPTER 3

An Unexpected Interlude; Dad Goes Fogging

Ernest Nicholson was another character in my young life. He was the husband of our Aunt Gladys, one of Mum's sisters. Mum referred to him as Uncle Ernest, but when Auntie spoke to us about him she referred to him as "your uncle 'Nick' " so that was what we came to call him. He was a bigger and taller man than Dad – about five feet eleven inches tall, at a guess. Whereas Dad used to go to work in overalls, Uncle Nick always wore a suit to work. Actually, he never spoke of going to *work*, but of going to *business*. One could not imagine him carrying out any kind of strenuous manual activity and I don't remember ever seeing him in anything other than one of his smart suits. He also used to wear 'spats' – which I thought looked very funny – to keep his shoes clean.

In his younger days Uncle Nick had served an apprenticeship to a watchmaker, which would have been in his home town of Spalding I believe. He married my Aunt Gladys in Lynn in 1934, when I was six. At that time he was employed by the then well-known King's Lynn watchmakers and jewellers, Burlinghams, in the High Street and this is where I remember him remaining throughout my boyhood.

Burlinghams shop was often used by Royalty when they were in residence at nearby Sandringham and Uncle would tell us about the various personages he had seen in the shop. In later years[1] he boasted that he had seen three queens in the shop at one and the same time. He was also proud of the fact that the firm was responsible for keeping in good repair all the many clocks in Sandringham House. He personally used to pay regular visits there to keep the clocks wound and adjusted.

Uncle was a refined looking chap - what my mother would probably have described as 'looking like a gentleman'. With his longish wavy hair swept back at the sides of his head he looked quite distinguished, I thought, quite different to Dad's short-back-and-sides style. Whilst walking down the street in his smart suit and spats, on meeting an acquaintance –

[1] *This would have been after the death of King George VI; the three queens would have been:- Queen Mary (widow of Geo.V); Queen Elizabeth (widow of Geo.VI. & known as the Queen Mother), and the present queen, Queen Elizabeth.*

especially a lady – he would give a suitable greeting and, at the same time, incline his head towards them and raise his trilby hat with a flourish, which looked most impressive.

Auntie Gladys and Uncle Nick were a childless couple and Auntie too was employed in the town. Each day, from Monday to Saturday, they would walk from their home at number twelve Keppel Street to their respective places of work: Uncle to Burlinghams in High Street; Auntie to Lowes Restaurant at number three Norfolk Street, where she was manageress. They both had Wednesday afternoons off, Wednesday being early closing day in the town.

Occasionally Auntie would have us round to Keppel Street at the weekend for tea. The distinctive feature of this, I remember, was of drinking tea out of Auntie's fine bone-china teacups; also the sweetened condensed milk she used in the tea instead of fresh milk – presumably to give us a treat. Uncle used to amuse us in a number of ways; when speaking affectionately to Auntie he would call her 'my duck', which struck me as very funny. Once, when Auntie had prepared a salad for tea that included some hard-boiled eggs, he enquired whether we all liked 'hen-fruit'.

Market Days

In the 1930s we had three market places in the town. The Tuesday Market Place, a large open space just beyond the northern end of the High Street, surrounded by a number of imposing buildings including the Corn Exchange and the Duke's Head Hotel, was the venue every week for many traders' stalls. I loved walking round the market with Dad, whenever I had the opportunity, to see what was on offer and, especially, to hear the traders' patter. There were fruit and vegetable stalls, seafood stalls, ones for tools, household goods, clothing, garden plants and virtually anything one could need.

One trader in particular who used to fascinate me was the man selling medical remedies. He would be surrounded by a crowd listening intently to his descriptions of the wonders of his various pills and potions.

I was amazed at all the ailments that could be cured, or avoided, by his wares. He had mixtures for coughs and colds, pills and salts for the liver, potions for sunburn, vapour rubs for the chest and treatments for any ache or pain you were likely to encounter. The persuasiveness of his patter was shown by the cash being handed over, in exchange for the little boxes and bottles he held up for display.

Another important market held on Tuesdays, was the Cattle market. One entrance to this was off Railway Road, just opposite Wellesley Street and near the northern end of Albion Street. As this was a very short distance from the railway station, beasts which were sent by rail were driven 'on the hoof' through the streets from the station and into the market. During this short walk they used to pass by the end of Kirby Street where we lived, then along Wellesley Street, before crossing Railway Road into the market. During school holidays we boys would often watch proceedings as the drovers herded their animals past the end of our street.

Grandad would sometimes take me into the market to look round the pens of cattle, pigs and sheep. Often he would meet someone he knew and would stop and chat to them. When this happened, rather than staying to listen to the conversation, I would ask him for permission to go into the building which contained the small wire cages in which were held the smaller animals that were to be auctioned. Here there would be all sorts of poultry: laying hens, point-of-lay pullets, guinea fowl, and bantams, plus some big colourful cockerels which would make their presence felt, every now and then, with a loud cock-a-doodle-do. The biggest attraction for me was, I think, the rabbits. There were big ones and small ones, long haired and short haired, erect ears and 'lop' ears, and as many colours as you could imagine – all making me fervently wish that I could have some rabbits of my own.

Actually, we must have been successful at one stage in persuading Dad to get us some rabbits, for I remember that for a while we had a couple in a wooden cage in our back yard. Dad used to take me on his bicycle on a Saturday afternoon into the countryside outside Lynn to collect green-food for them. I don't think that we can have had them for very long for I don't remember much about them. Putting two and two together, I can only imagine that it must have been during a period when Dad had a vegetable allotment, somewhere near the station. There he would have been able to take the manure when the rabbit cage was cleaned out; otherwise, as we had no garden, there would have been no-where to dispose of it.

As I watched proceedings in the small-animals shed, it was very entertaining to see the auctioneer doing his job. His loud patter would go ahead like an express train and I could hardly understand a word he said – and I could not see how any of the buyers could either. However, every so often his hammer would come smartly down on his board and, apparently, a cage of animals had been sold. I would be so engrossed in all this that time would be forgotten, until I would feel a tap on my shoulder from Grandad who had decided it was time to 'be drawin' on'.

The other market in the town was the Saturday one, held at the end of St James' Street, on the space alongside St. Margaret's church, just beyond the southern end of the High Street. Unlike the Tuesday market, the Saturday one was quite small, just a few stalls, and therefore by comparison not seeming so attractive to me.

An Unexpected Interlude

Mum was not always in the best of health in our young days. We children didn't know what her medical problems were; we just accepted the fact that she had them and was sometimes 'under the doctor'. Our GP was Dr Dummere, whose surgery was on London Road. I remember Mum commenting on how understanding the doctor was in his willingness to wait for his payments. It could not have been easy, with three children to support, to pay medical bills in addition to the normal family expenses, on Dad's railway wage of just over two pounds per week.

At one point, whilst we were still quite young – I think I was about nine at the time – Mum's ill-health brought about an unexpected, and unpleasant, break in our normal family life. The doctor had insisted that Mum must have a time of complete rest. But this, of course, was not possible while she had three children to look after. We had none of today's modern household conveniences in those days and looking after a family like ours was a full-time job. The result of the doctor's decision, therefore, was that we children would have to be fostered out for a time – a very unpleasant prospect, we felt.

Knowing how impecunious was the family at that time, I just cannot imagine how this fostering arrangement was to be financed; it remains a mystery to me to this day. Dad, I know, was a member of The Ancient Order of Foresters' Friendly Society. He used to pay a few pence a week into this organisation which, if he was off work owing to sickness – luckily a rare occurrence – would provide him with a benefit of about ten shillings a week. But, I don't think that the Society made any provision for the financing of such an emergency as Dad was obviously facing at this time. However, he obviously managed it somehow, for it was arranged for Geoff and me to stay with a Mr and Mrs Dye, who lived in the town.

The Dyes could accommodate us two boys, but they were not able to have our little sister Joan as well. Fortunately, some helpful Kirby Street neighbours – a Mr and Mrs Gore, at number five – stepped in and offered to look after her. As things turned out, the Gores became very fond of Joan whilst she was in their care and, later, this kindly couple were to become close and lasting friends of the family; we got to calling them 'Auntie Elsie and Uncle Billa'.

I don't know who had put our parents in touch with Mr and Mrs Dye, the couple who were to have Geoff and me; to my knowledge, they had not been acquainted with them previously. The Dye's home was a first floor flat above a butcher's shop, located on the corner of Tower Street and Blackfriars Street at Baxters Plain. From one of their windows one could look out onto the nearby Majestic Cinema. Geoff and I were very apprehensive about going there, but we need not have been so worried, for the Dyes turned out to be a homely middle-aged couple who did their best to put us at ease. Our stay there was to be reasonably happy in the circumstances. An entertaining feature of their home was the talking parrot that they owned and which lived in a large cage in the living room. It was very amusing listening to the parrot and trying to teach it to say new words.

The flat above the butcher's shop (now Antonio's Wine Bar). Author.

Whilst staying at the flat we used to walk to school each day as usual. During the school day it was easy to forget that we were living away from home, but evenings were more difficult. Apart from the parrot, a little conversation with the Dyes, or listening to the wireless when they had it on, there was not much to keep our minds off home, and Mum and Dad. The worst times were bedtimes. One Saturday morning, with my feeling of homesickness becoming ever stronger, I decided that I would call in at home to find out how much longer we were to be a way.

Slipping away from the flat just after breakfast, without saying where I was going, I walked to Kirby Street. On entering the house I found both Mum and Dad there, which surprised me, for I had expected that Dad would have been at work – he must have been having a day off. They were sitting at the table, still having breakfast and, as I looked at them there, I was overcome with a wave of desolation – a feeling of having lost my place at that intimate table.   My parents, seeing my distress, comforted me. After I had somewhat recovered they explained that Mum was now feeling much better; that I had to be patient for a while longer and that then we would soon all be at home, together again.   Now, feeling more composed after having been reassured that the family would all soon be united again, I managed to say good-by and took myself back to the Dye's flat.

About another week passed; then, as had been promised, Geoff and I were able to go back home. Joan also returned from the Gore's. Before very long family life resumed its normal routine, as if nothing untoward had ever happened, and we were all happy again.   Fortunately this family dispersion never had to be repeated and, for the rest of our childhood in Lynn, Mum was able to cope fairly well with her problems

Dad's 'Fogging' Duties

The un-social hours of Dad's carriage-cleaning job was an accepted part of life and the routine was only broken occasionally during bad weather when we had fog; then he would be called out for fog-signalling duties – or "fogging" as the men used to call it. In thick fog the railway signals could become invisible to the locomotive crews. The signalling system therefore needed to be backed up with some means of ensuring that the engine-men knew the positions were showing 'all clear' or were at 'danger'. On today's railways where most of the signals are of the modern colour-light type, fog does not cause such problems. In the 1930s the signals were of the old semaphore kind and were lit only with oil-lamps, which were unable to penetrate thick fog or heavy snow. A back up to the main signalling system was provided by the 'fog-signal-men'.

One such winter evening remains distinctly in my memory. We had finished our tea and were listening to the wireless. Dad went outside to the coal-shed in the back yard to fill the scuttle for making up our living room fire for the evening. On coming back in again, he said to Mum:

"Would you make me up some sandwiches while I get myself ready – I shall have to go fogging". Now my Mum hated Dad having to go out on this cold, damp and lonely job and her reaction was predictable: "Why don't you wait and see if they come to call you out – perhaps the fog will soon clear" she said. But, having seen how thick was the fog outside, Dad knew that to wait would only delay the inevitable call-out.

Mum therefore packed up sandwiches for at least two or three snacks – for there was no telling when he would be back – and after changing into his working clothes Dad set off for the station. Obviously, the prospect of a cold, wet night out in the fog was not something to relish, but Dad never complained about his lot. In any case, his basic wage of just over two pounds a week was not much on which to support a family and any overtime, such as fogging provided, must have been very welcome. Whilst Mum detested these fogging interludes, my brother and I found them intriguing.

I used to imagine Dad out there all alone in the fog helping to keep the railway safe and I would ply him with questions about the job. His replies taught me some of the facts about railway signalling and of the functions of a 'fog-man'. The vast majority of the signals were of the semaphore type – a semaphore arm on a post. During daylight hours, the position of the arm informed the train driver whether the line ahead was clear, or whether he had to stop at the signal. A horizontal aspect of the arm, i.e. at right angles to the post, denoted 'Danger – Stop'; this was the normal position of the arm. When the signalman 'pulled off' the signal so that the arm was inclined at an angle of about 45 degrees to the post, it told the driver: 'All Clear – Go Ahead'

During hours of darkness, when the signal arm could not be seen, the problem was overcome by two large spectacle glasses, one red and the other green incorporated into the pivoting end of the arm. When the arm is horizontal, a red light shows for 'Danger'; when the arm is lowered (or raised) to the 45 degree angle, then a green light shows through the spectacle for 'All Clear'. An oil lamp fixed to the signal post, just behind the spectacle glasses provides the light itself. This works well during fine weather, but in the event of thick fog neither the signal arm by day, nor the red or green lights by night, could be seen by the trainmen and this was when the alternative fog-signalling arrangements came into play.

The arranging of these 'fogging' duties was a well-organised affair. The men involved were drawn from a number of different station staff who could be spared from their normal tasks. They would include porters, platelayers, carriage cleaners and others. Their names and addresses, together with details such as the position of the particular signal post which each man was responsible for, were recorded on lists in the stationmaster's office and in the signal-boxes, making it possible for the fog-men to be called without delay whenever this was necessary. It was in fact the men's duty, whenever they became aware of thick fog, or heavy snow, whether or not they were on, or off, duty, to report to the signalman in the signal-box which controlled their particular signal. They would collect an allocation of detonators, a hand lamp with sliding coloured glasses – which corresponded with the signal lights - and some coloured flags.

On arriving at their signal each man's duty was to indicate to the train-crews the current position of the signal. When the signal shows 'Danger', he places a detonator on the track to denote this to the crews and also shows a red light with his hand-lamp. When the signalman pulls off the signal to 'all clear' the detonator is removed and a green hand-lamp signal is shown until the train has gone through. As soon as the train has passed and the signal goes back to its normal position of 'danger', the detonator is replaced on the line, and his hand-lamp changed to show a red light, and so on ad infinitum, as long as the fog lasts.

Somebody, such as a ganger would be responsible for keeping the fog-men supplied with detonators and would also occasionally relieve each fog-man so that he could have his food. Dad would take the opportunity during these short breaks to eat his sandwiches and have a brief warm-up in front of the little coal fire in the nearest plate-layers' hut. If the fog persisted he could be stuck on the job for twelve, fifteen hours or so, in which case more food would have to be sent to him. Mum would prepare this and deliver it to the station, to be passed on to Dad.

The Tramp

During the nineteen-thirties we sometimes used to see men known as 'tramps': people who for various reasons, either through force of circumstances or by choice, had given up a settled life to wander round the countryside. They would raise the little money they needed, either by doing the odd day's work – perhaps on a farm – or often by begging. One Saturday morning, one such man made his way along the Kirby Street houses, knocking at doors and begging to be given a little cash. On answering his knock at the door, Mum took one look at his tattered clothes, at the cloth bundle he was carrying – which appeared to hold all his worldly possessions – and immediately felt sorry for him. Asking him to wait, she disappeared into the kitchen.

As the man stood at the open door, we children looked at him with wide-eyed amazement; we had never seen anyone looking so dirty or with clothes in such a terrible state. His face was grimed with dirt, his hair matted, his filthy clothes were torn and full of holes. That someone could be in such a state and look as bad as he did, was completely new to us. After a few minutes Mum came from the kitchen with a small package of sandwiches which she handed to the tramp. Stuffing this into the torn remains of one of his coat pockets, he thanked her and bade her good day.

Once the front door was shut again, we couldn't contain our questions about the tramp. Mum explained that people can fall upon bad times and end up like the man we had just seen; that we should feel sorry for them and help them if we could. 'Why did you make him some sandwiches, when he asked for money?' we asked. She told us that some of these men got into a 'drink' habit; they didn't eat properly and were only interested in obtaining money with which to buy more drink, which was not good for them.

Geoff and I were still intrigued by this weird character and went outside to play in the street – secretly hoping to see more of the tramp and what he was doing. He was not to be seen at the top half of the street, so he had obviously ended his stint of knocking on doors. But when we looked the other way, beyond where the houses ended, we spotted him sitting on the ground in the sun, leaning back on the 'wood-yard' fence. We watched as he pulled the packet of sandwiches from his pocket, unwrapped them and munched his way through the first sandwich. Then, the warm sunshine seemed to make him sleepy, for he stopped eating and his head dropped down onto his chest.

We watched the tramp, thinking that he had gone off to sleep, but after a few moments he came to again and lifted his head up. Suddenly, glancing down at the sandwiches, he scooped them up in his fist, hurled them over his head and they disappeared over the top of the fence behind him. Then, getting slowly to his feet, he walked off down the street and we lost sight of him as he rounded the corner at the end. Geoff and I were highly incensed to think what the tramp had done with Mum's specially made sandwiches and we rushed indoors again to report to her. Mum was quite philosophical about the incident, but we complained about it to each other for some time. Looking back, the event provided us with one or two new experiences in the 'school of life'.

CHAPTER 4

Boyish Activities and the 'Best Laid Plans'...

Whist we were very young, outdoor play was restricted to our small back yard, but Mum was quite resourceful in keeping us amused. I remember the trouble she went to contrive a makeshift tent for us by hanging two old bed sheets on the clothesline, stretching them out one on each side and securing them along the bottom with a few bricks. With an old rug and a stool inside, we were able to amuse ourselves for hours with our pretend camp.

There was very little motor traffic around in those days, especially through streets like Kirby Street, and it was the custom for the local children to play in the street and, by about the time we reached school age we were joining in. A favourite game, especially of the girls, was skipping. With one of them at each end turning the long rope, quite a number of people could take part at the same time. Some became very skilful at joining in the skipping whilst the rope was actually turning. In addition to the street itself the wilder 'wood-yard' area, previously mentioned, was used for playing games such as hide-and-seek, or cowboys-and-Indians, amongst the vegetation.

On wet days a favourite indoor game for Geoff and me was playing with our toy farm animals. These animals, manufactured by Messrs. Britains, made of painted lead, were very realistic. The small ones such as pigs and sheep, cost one penny each and the bigger ones, the cows and horses, cost two pence each. When we had saved our spare pennies we would pay a visit to Woolworths in the High Street to increase our stock. Other items one could buy were incidentals such as gates, trees, milk churns, etc.

We would set everything on the kitchen table. First was to arrange the farm layout. For the field boundaries we formed hedges made of wool that had been undone and salvaged by Mum from old jumpers and cardigans. Using various greens and browns, and bunching the wool up, the hedges looked very realistic. A farm roadway would be formed through the middle, with gates giving access into the field on either side. The finishing touch would be a farmyard at one end, with blocks of wood to denote the buildings. With the basic layout made, the different animals could be set out in the fields, cows brought in for milking, pigs sent to market, lambing attended to and anything else which imagination suggested needed doing on the farm. This would all keep us occupied for hours; I think that both Geoff and I, at this time, had decided that when we became 'grown-up' we would be farmers.

Woodworking Aspirations: One Christmas I was given a set of junior carpentry tools. This fired my imagination and I began to think about all the things I would make. Being impatient to begin using the tools I pestered Mum about getting some wood. She took me into the back yard and, giving me a length of wood she managed to find in the shed, suggested that I knock in some nails and pull them out again with the pincers. At this, I remember, I was highly indignant. Fancy expecting that I – who had been imagining such wonderful things I could make – should be content to knock nails into an old lump of wood and then simply pull them out again! Mum, of course, realised that a small boy with his first set of tools could not run before he could walk; but I, remembering the enjoyment of my carpentry efforts at Grandad's, was very impatient.

I began to think of how I could get more wood. When the following Saturday came and I received from Dad my regular 'Saturday Penny' I hurried down to the bottom of the street to the Hallack & Bond warehouse. I had often noticed stacks of empty wooden boxes in their yard, so I asked the first man I found whether I could buy a penny worth of wood. He asked me what I wanted it for and I told him I wanted it for making something with my tools. The man was quite helpful, found me a nice box and for good measure put more loose pieces of wood inside it. Quite delighted, I hurried home with my prize. The rest of the day was spent in the back yard, cutting and nailing pieces of wood to make model aeroplanes.

This little venture proved to be the start of quite a useful little hobby that would keep me occupied whenever life failed to provide any more immediately pressing boyish projects. From then on, whenever I ran out of material I would repeat the visit to Hallack & Bond's warehouse and my request for wood was usually rewarded. One of my carpentry undertakings was the construction of a home for a couple of pet mice. The two black mice were given to me by an older girl from across the street. My mouse house turned out quite well, but unfortunately my mouse-keeping efforts were not so successful: I had not understood the need for regular daily feeding and, on looking to see why the mice had not appeared for a couple of days in the wire-fronted section of their house, I discovered them dead in the bedroom end.

Friends: As time went by Geoff and I felt as free as the birds and used to roam and ramble locally at will. Sometimes there would be just the two of us; at others we would play with our own particular friend. Mine was Peter Adams, a boy about a year older than me, who lived at number two at the top of the street. His father was a boot and shoe repairer and had a little workshop behind their house. Peter had an older brother who had left school and was working, so he was much more affluent than mere schoolboys like us. One Saturday his brother offered to pay Peter tuppence to clean his bicycle for him.

Peter asked me to help him with the cleaning for a share of the reward, which I agreed to. The dirtiest parts of the bike were the wheels. Taking one of these each we busily pulled strips of old cloths backwards and forwards round the wheel hubs and between the spokes, quite a fiddly job. After some time the bike looked quite respectable and, after an inspection by its owner, we were duly paid a penny each. This was very welcome for it effectively doubled my allowance that week, of my normal 'Saturday' penny which I used to receive from Dad. Sweets were my usual purchases; you could get about five toffees for a halfpenny, I remember. A 'Milky Way' chocolate bar cost one penny and a 'Mars Bar' two pence.

Geoff's main friend at the time was a lad nicknamed 'Pip'. Pip's surname was Marshall and he lived in a nearby street. Geoff would invite him round to our house, where they would often amuse themselves with drawing, which Pip was very good at. He was adept at copying characters from children's comics and I was quite envious of his skill in creating such recognisable likenesses of people such as Pop-eye, Desperate Dan, Key-hole Kate and other well-known characters. Another of his skills was the making of model aeroplanes, using 'smarties' tubes. Mum, I remember, quite approved of 'Pip' who was a fairly quiet and thoughtful boy. She was not so sure about Peter who was much more lively and boisterous – I think that she thought he could possibly lead me astray.

As I look back to those days of the 1930s, I feel that we were very fortunate in the amount of freedom we had. It is sad to reflect that in today's world we no longer feel comfortable to allow our children the liberty that we enjoyed. This is partly due of course to the great increase in the volume and speed of today's traffic. The most regrettable reason, though, is the unmistakable increase in the number of questionable people around today. In the '30s paedophiles were unheard of. Most young boys then were keen on collecting cigarette cards, one of which used to be contained in every cigarette packet. It was a normal thing, when you spotted a man smoking, to approach him and to ask if he had a card to give you – I did it many scores of times. What a sad state of affairs when we have to teach our children to be suspicious of strangers!

Broken Biscuits and a Picnic at the Sandpits: If we became bored with activities around Kirby Street and wanted a change, a favourite destination was the Wootton Woods and the 'Sandpits'. These were about three and a half miles from home, between South Wootton and Castle Rising. Before going we would persuade Mum to pack us up a picnic. This would usually consist of bread and butter, some hard-boiled eggs and, if we were lucky, some little chocolate covered cream cakes. For drink we would have bottles of orange squash. If she had no cakes for us, Mum would give us a penny and send us to buy a pennorth of broken biscuits at the nearby Co-operative store in Norfolk Street.

If there were few customers waiting in the shop we would be back home with the biscuits within a few minutes. Sometimes there would be a number of ladies doing their grocery shopping, which could mean a longer wait for us until the grown-ups had been served. However, this didn't normally bother us for the Co-op was an interesting sort of shop and there would be plenty of activity to keep us amused. Items were not pre-packed in those days – you asked for the amounts you required and they were weighed up for you at the counter.

Butter, for instance, would be a big bulk lump on a marble slab at the back of the counter. Two hand-held wooden butter 'pats' would be used to separate a piece of about the right size and this would be patted into a neat shape on the slab. Then, by holding one wooden pat on each side of it, the butter would be lifted deftly onto a piece of greaseproof paper and plopped onto the scales for weighing. Rarely did it differ by more than a small fraction from the amount that the customer had asked for.

The bacon slicer was another interesting piece of equipment. A large piece of bacon on the machine would be cut into slices by a revolving circular blade. I liked to watch the assistant as she deftly caught the slices as they were cut off by the blade, and quickly laid each piece onto the waiting paper before catching the next slice. Sugar too was weighed up at the counter and supplied in thick blue paper bags.

Co-operative Society customers were given a numbered 'dividend' account and each of their purchases counted towards the build-up of dividend to which they would eventually be entitled. The payout of this, I think, took place annually. I seem to remember that Mum would draw her entitlement just before Christmas and I can well imagine that the dividend must have been a great boon to many a hard-up family in those days.

Whenever a purchase was made, the counter assistant would record its value, together with the customer's dividend number, on small tickets contained in a pad kept on the counter. The cash and tickets would then be sent to the cashier's office, located on a higher floor, to be recorded. A copy-ticket, plus any change due, would then be returned to the assistant to hand to the customer for her own record. Whenever Mum sent us to the shop for groceries she would remind us to make sure that we quoted her 'divi' number and in time we got to know the number by heart.

For me, the fascinating aspect of all this was the actual apparatus by means of which all this transferring of cash and tickets to and from the office was done. The official name of the equipment I didn't know, but it reminded me of the London Underground Tube system. It was composed of a network of tubes, of approximately two and a half inches diameter, through which the cash was transported. Parts of this tubing extended down to various convenient points behind the shop counters, each with an access flap near the bottom. The assistants put the money and tickets into a special canister and inserted this through the access flap, into the pipe. Canister and contents, by travelling through the pipe, were whisked up to the office above. After a short wait, the canister would arrive back at the counter, for retrieval of ticket and change to hand to the customer.

However, I return to our reason for this particular visit to the shop — broken biscuits. Even biscuits were not pre-packed in those days but came to the shop in large square bulk tins, from which they were dispensed in paper bags. Each tin was decorated with a mouth-watering illustration of the variety it contained and a row of these tins would stand on view on a shelf at the back of the counter. But, as we knew, it would not be from those tins that our requested broken biscuits would be taken. The assistant would dive under the counter and retrieve some tins that had earlier been emptied of saleable whole biscuits and now contained only broken remnants. She would take these pieces from the various tins and put them into a paper bag for us. Many of them were fair sized pieces and usually we would receive a good bag full and a number of different varieties. So, pleased with our penny purchase, we would hurry home for the biscuits to be added to our picnic preparations.

When the picnic had been fairly apportioned by Mum and, together with our bottles of drink, stowed in our bags, we were at last ready to set off for our intended destination: the Sandpits and Wootton Woods. Very occasionally for these jaunts, if we had the pennies, we would catch the bus at 'Townsend's Corner' and ride as far as South Wootton, then walk the rest of the way from there. Usually though, even if we had the fare – which often we hadn't – we would decide to walk the whole three and a bit miles so that we could save our precious pennies for other things.

On one such occasion, we had walked through Gaywood and were somewhere on the Wootton Road, when we were approached by a little black cat that was making a loud and persistent mewing and started to follow us. We both became very concerned about the cat, for it was as thin as a rake and seemed to be starving. The more noise the cat made, the more we felt sorry for it and one of us suggested that perhaps we could buy a little milk for it. After raiding our pockets to see whether we had enough cash, Geoff went into a little shop we came to on the left-hand side of the road whilst I stayed with the cat. Shortly after he emerged from the shop successfully carrying a half-pint bottle of milk. But, now we had an unforeseen problem: what could we pour the milk into in order to feed the cat?

The only thing we saw lying around was a discarded carrier bag[2] lying in the gutter, which at first sight didn't appear of any use. However, one of us had a bright idea as to how we could use it – which one of us it was I cannot now recall. The thick paper bag was laid on the ground and a depression made in it, into which we could pour some milk and, very shortly the cat's tongue was going 'nineteen-to-the-dozen', lapping it up. Though we lost some of the milk onto the ground, we managed to get quite a bit into the cat and were quite pleased with our achievement.

We left the cat whilst it was still drinking and started on our way once more, both with a warm glow inside, I think, and quite proud that we had been able to help the poor cat. But then things went wrong; we got to discussing the cash – and there was a bit of confusion about who had actually paid for the milk, or how much each had paid. The argument became rather heated and, though it must have lasted a minute or two, fortunately did not come to blows. It was not so much the actual cash

[2] *The carrier bags supplied by shops in those days, unlike the polythene ones supplied by the supermarkets today, but were made of thick brown paper, with string handles.*

that was worrying us, I think, but rather who should take the main credit for the good deed done for the cat. Anyway, eventually remembering why we were on the Wootton road in the first place, we forgot our differences and continued on our walk.

From this point we would shortly pass the New Inn on our left and just beyond that, the South Wootton crossroads. Here, in the middle of the road used to be a small circular green, which the local service buses between Lynn and South Wootton used as a terminus before returning to Lynn. The left-hand road led to the village, the right-hand one was the Hillington road and, ahead, the old A149 went on through Castle Rising village towards Hunstanton. Today, of course, South Wootton and Castle Rising have been by-passed and this section of road from Wootton, as far as Babingley, has been downgraded. It has given up its A149 number to the new by-pass, starting at the Hardwick roundabout.

As we boys passed over the crossroads we would keep a lookout on chance of seeing an AA patrolman. The Automobile Association had one of their telephone boxes here, standing on the Lynn side of the junction. This box, all black except for the yellow panels at the top on which their logo was displayed, used to seem rather mysterious and I wondered what was inside it. Sometimes a patrolman's three-wheeled motorcycle combination would be parked outside the box with the patrolman either inside the box, or standing alongside, watching the passing traffic.

Instead of a passenger sidecar, the motorcycle had a large squat box at the side, tapered at the front rather like the bows of a ship. The box, I was told, contained tools and spare parts that might be needed for the helping of AA motorist members out of trouble. The vehicle was resplendent in the AA yellow and with the logo painted on the side of the toolbox. The rider too was very smart, in khaki uniform, with breeches, gaiters and peaked cap. His job, I thought, must be quite exciting – riding the highways on his smart steed, on the lookout for broken-down motorists in need of assistance.

Striking out from here along the Hunstanton road, we had only about another mile and a quarter to walk before reaching our destination. The place we used to know as the 'Sandpits' was located on the left-hand side and quite close to the road. Whether or not there had previously been some sort of sand workings there, I don't know; there was none taking place there when we were boys. Basically the area was just a sandy slope. This 'hill', though not huge, was steep enough and tall enough, with its surface of loose sand, to need quite a bit of energy to walk or run up to its top. It was certainly exhilarating to run down from top to bottom. This area, together with the surrounding woodland, was a wonderful place for youngsters to play in.

The 'Sandpits' & Wootton Woods. Author.

Here in imagination we could cross the sand of the Sahara desert on our camels, be explorers in the jungles of Africa, or be cowboys and Indians in the 'wild-west.' Over the top of the sandy slope, after entering a little way into the woods there was a sort of track or bridle-way. This was about six feet wide, with a row of tall conifer trees along one side; the ground on the other side sloped down into a lower part of the wood. We nicknamed this pathway 'The Trail' and would gallop along it on our imaginary horses. Down in the lower part of the trees was a tiny stream – so small that I suppose it barely deserved to be called a stream – but to us it was a make-believe river where we could water our horses.

After a busy afternoon's play in this, our favourite place, it would be time to attend to the messages by now coming from our stomachs: to sit down and eat our picnic. The chosen place for this was usually a grassy knoll in some trees, just over the top of the sand hill. After eating our bread and butter and hard-boiled eggs, plus the broken biscuits, with gusto, the realisation would dawn that perhaps it was time to pack up and go home. So tired, but happy – but after a last run down the sand-hill – we would start on our three-mile plus trudge back to Kirby Street.

Fishing: Once, during the summer school holidays, Geoff and I went fishing. This incident I now recall with amusement – though I doubt whether Geoff remembers it as funny. We had been given a fishing net each: those little nets that are held open by a wire and attached to the end of a long cane. So, having the equipment and being impatient to put it to use, we decided we would try our hands at a fishing expedition. We set off from home with our nets, plus a two-pound jam jar each which had been provided by Mum, in which to hold the expected catch. The jars had been carefully tied round with string beneath the rims and with loops over the top to act as handles.

We made our way to 'The Walks': an area of park-land in which were a number of tree-lined avenues, or 'Walks' as they are known in Lynn, and through which runs a little river. The spot we selected for our fishing pitch was where the river ran parallel, and fairly close to the 'Broad Walk', behind the old Lynn and West Norfolk hospital. The water here, I would guess to have been about fifteen to twenty inches deep and, as we peered in we could see, every so often, small shoals of little fish darting backwards and forwards. This was exciting and we thought that we should be putting fish in our jars in no time at all. But we had underestimated their agility. We found also that it was difficult to move the nets very quickly in the water, so just as we tried to net the fish they would turn and dart away with incredible speed.

We persevered for some time but without success; it was most frustrating. Suddenly, Geoff, who had been standing up and leaning forward over the edge, overbalanced and fell into the water. He was soaked from head to toe. I grabbed his hand and pulled him, dripping, onto the bank. 'Oh dear, now we are in for it, especially me', I thought. Mum always regarded Geoff as rather a delicate boy and, though I was only one year older, she tended to look upon me as responsible for his welfare when we were out. What was I to do? Bringing all my boyish resourcefulness to bear I came up with a plan. It was a lovely hot, sunny day; I would get Geoff dry before we went home and nobody need know anything about the matter. Nearby, on the far side of the 'Broad Walk' was a long open area of grass, part of the recreation ground, in full sunshine and just right for my plan.

Taking charge, I ordered him to walk backwards and forwards over the grass so that he would dry in the sun. My boyish logic told me that the sun would have its fullest effect if he walked slowly, so I told him to walk as slowly as he possibly could. I must have convinced Geoff of the wisdom of my plan, for without any argument he started to wander slowly backwards and forwards across the grass. I sat down at the edge of the grass, near the old Red Mount Chapel, and watched Geoff as he slowly crossed and re-crossed the length of the recreation ground. Just what a passer-by would have thought to see a dripping wet boy wandering like a tortoise and another one sitting and watching him, I don't know; but luckily, so far I had not seen anyone. Geoff continued plodding on and I kept faith in my clever drying scheme.

But, as Robbie Burns said: "The best laid schemes o' mice and men gang oft a-gley". Long before my plan had a chance to come to fruition, who should come along but a Kirby Street neighbour, a large, stern-looking woman, who had taken in the situation at a glance. My explanations went unheeded. Grabbing Geoff by the arm, and with me bringing up the rear with the fishing gear, she marched us home and presented us to Mother. The indignity of being hauled off home like this was bad enough for my pride. It was made worse, on arrival, when Mum told me that my drying idea had been "hare-brained" and that I should have taken Geoff home immediately.   I've never been keen on fishing since!

Pea Picking: *My* friend Peter was a little older than me and more experienced in the ways of the world; very often, the boyish expeditions, which we two embarked on, were suggested by him.   One Saturday morning he announced that he was going pea picking to earn some money and he asked me to go with him.   I had no idea what to do or where to go to become a pea-picker, but Peter was quite confident about it and had obviously been before.   The thought of earning some cash to extend my purchasing power was very tempting and I agreed to go with him.

We set out and walked along London Road, and then on through South Lynn until we came to the 'Cut Bridge' which spanned the river to the south-west of the town.   The bridge had five high concrete arches rising up along each side of the bridge: three big ones in the middle and a slightly smaller one at each end.   On reaching the nearest of the arches Peter, instead of keeping to the foot-way alongside it, started to climb up the arch itself, shouting to me: 'Come on – we'll go over the top'. 'We can't do that!' I answered. 'Course we can said Peter', without stopping. Dubiously I followed him onto the arch and carefully crept up the concrete until I was about a third of the way up.   But, on looking down and seeing how far below the water looked, I got cold feet and gingerly backed down again.   Meanwhile, in his daredevil way Peter had disappeared over the top and made his way down the other side!

Once over the bridge I was on unfamiliar territory, but Peter continued on quite self-assured. Whether we took the Wisbech road or the Sutton Bridge one I cannot now recall, but we had not gone very far when a motor lorry caught us up from behind. To my surprise, Peter confidently held up his hand and signalled to the driver, who brought the lorry to a stop alongside us. After exchanging a few words with Peter, he invited us to hop in. It turned out that, as anticipated by Peter, the lorry was in fact on its way to the pea field and the driver had guessed where we were heading for.

Peter quickly jumped in and I followed. Unfortunately for me, before I was settled the door swung to and momentarily trapped my little finger between it and the doorpost. Looking at my finger as the door swung open again I had a shock; although the skin had not been broken the finger looked a funny colour and there was a deep indentation all round the top joint. I felt faint and settled back in the seat to nurse myself as the driver re-started the lorry. By the time we arrived at the pea field the pain had subsided a little and the finger looked more normal so, with not knowing what to expect from this new pea picking experience, I managed to forget the finger and to concentrate on what was going on around me.

There were a lot of people already in the field busily picking. The two men in charge looked at us two boys rather doubtfully, I thought, but decided to take us on. We were each supplied with a willow basket and a hessian sack and told that the pay was one shilling and three pence per sack-full. We were shown where to start and we settled down to pick. But, judging by the time it took me to fill the basket, it was going to take me ages to fill that enormous sack I thought. However, 1/3d was also an enormous sum – the equivalent of fifteen weeks pocket money – so with that happy thought I plodded on.

It was hours later, when Peter who had filled his sack whist mine was still only two-thirds full, went off to have it checked and to collect his pay. A few minutes later he was back and looking rather sheepish – with a less than full sack – and started picking again in order to fill it. Apparently he had succumbed to temptation and had stuffed some pea haulm into his sack, but had been found out when the sack was weighed and he had been told off. As things turned out we both completed the sack filling at about the same time and went off to collect our reward; Peter obviously embarrassed and a little red-faced, remembering his earlier ticking-off. Whether we managed to get a lift part of the way home, I can't recall; but I do remember the feeling of having that small fortune of a shilling piece and three pennies in my trouser pocket!

New Job and New House
Life went on fairly routinely until about mid-1938, I think it was, when two changes for the family took place: Dad changed his job - and we moved to another house. Giving up the carriage cleaning, Dad became a porter at the railway station. Family finances were never discussed with us children, but we were well aware that money was quite short and I have a feeling therefore that these two changes were financially connected. The higher wage of the new portering job would have made the move to a larger house, with its higher rent, more affordable. So, leaving Kirby Street we moved into No.4 Metcalfe Avenue, a semi-detached three bed-roomed council house in South Lynn.

My sister Joan was delighted that she could now have her own bedroom. Another advantage of the house was that all three bedrooms had their own access from the landing area; we no longer had to go through one bedroom to reach another one. Further wonders we found upstairs were a bathroom and an indoor lavatory. The old tin bath, the night-time under-bed chamber pots, the daytime trips to the toilet at the end of the backyard, all previously needed at Kirby Street, had suddenly become obsolete!

A further improvement was that when entering the house one did not walk straight into the front room; there was a little hallway inside the front door. Doors in the hall led, on the one side into a large sitting room, and on the other into a small dining room and with the kitchen behind this. In the kitchen was a brick-built copper, very much like the old Kirby Street one, but with the convenience of being indoors. This could be used both for doing the weekly wash and for heating bath water. The clever part about the latter use, was that when the water was ready it did not, any longer, have to be carried to the bath: it was pumped up to the bathroom by means of a hand-pump which was located on the wall just above the copper. We had never known such modern conveniences!

The house was surrounded on three sides by garden: a small piece in the front, plus sizeable pieces at the side and the back. What a change this was from the small concrete back yard, which we had left behind. Dad intended to grow vegetables on the side area and the plan was to have some lawn behind the house for us children to play on – quite exciting for us. After we had moved in, uncle 'Sid' – husband of our Aunt Julia, one of Mum's sisters – came to help Dad dig over the garden. I never really liked Uncle Sid, regarding him as rather a 'know-all'. He himself had lived in a council house now for a number of years and regarded himself as an expert on the subject. I remember him telling Dad that although our bathroom was glazed with frosted glass; we would nevertheless need to have curtains up at the window. He also commented that some new tenants had no idea what the bath was used for, but thought that it was for storing coal in. This comment I treated with a pinch of salt – after all, I thought, why on earth would people take coal to store upstairs, when the fires it was needed for were downstairs!

Unfortunately, very soon after moving in, the family's excitement with the new house was spoilt by the finding of an unpleasant smell in the kitchen. Mum in particular was worried about it and when a search revealed that the smell was caused by an infestation of cockroaches, she was horrified. Obviously, the bugs had been attracted by food and warmth in the house during the tenancy of previous occupants. The council landlords were contacted urgently and we received visits from one of their workmen to deal with the problem. I cannot now remember what method he used to get rid of the creatures, but eventually the house was cleared of the cockroaches and Mum's enjoyment of her new home was restored.

CHAPTER 5

Wider Concerns; Changes Thick and Fast

Whilst these little family affairs were taking place, much wider concerns were unfolding. I well remember the apprehension felt by my parents at the time about the probability that Britain was going to find itself embroiled in a war with Nazi Germany; also their relief at the report that the prime minister, Mr Chamberlain, had signed an agreement with Adolf Hitler. The threat of war had, it seemed, been averted. But, the resulting feeling of relief did not last. In the following year, 1939, it became more and more obvious that war was inevitable and, at 11am on the 3rd September there came the climax of all the suspense. Once more we were at war with Germany.

In a strange sort of way this knowledge, I think, brought a kind of relief in itself: though the thing people had dreaded had happened, the suspense was broken and they now knew what to expect. The immediate fear now, was of air attacks by the German air force on our towns and cities, which prompted the authorities to quickly put air raid precautions (A.R.P.) in place. One of the actions taken was called the 'blackout' – the avoidance of showing any light during hours of darkness, which could assist enemy bombers to find their targets. Street lights were all extinguished, house-holders instructed that no light whatsoever must be allowed to show from their windows, and motorists were to make do with much reduced light from heavily masked headlights.

I have since learned that, at the very start of the blackout, the use of vehicle headlights was completely banned; that it was only after this resulted in a vast increase in road deaths that the compromise of allowing masked lighting was allowed. The masks were made from thin sheets of metal shaped to fit over the headlamp glass, with a few narrow horizontal slits cut out, so as to allow through a small amount of light onto the road ahead. Smaller versions of these were made for use on cycle lamps – a plate placed over the glass and held in place by the screw-on rim of the lamp. I did not possess a bicycle in 1939 but later, from 1942 when I started work, I used one of these covers on my cycle lamp until the end of the war.

Some special blackout material, a black cotton fabric, was made available in the shops, some of which Mum obtained for covering our windows. The material was attached to some wooden frames that were made up by Dad, to fit tightly between our window reveals. The lifting of these frames in and out of the windows became a night and morning routine; during the day they were placed against the walls behind the furniture.

Air Raid Wardens were appointed and very soon made their presence felt. One duty they carried out very assiduously was to check for any light showing from house windows and one evening we received a knock on the door from a very officious sounding chap. Dad, without switching on the hall light for fear of showing light outside, opened the door to him. "Do you know your light is showing?" barked the warden. Dad went outside with him to be shown the offending light. The complaint was about a tiny pinprick of light showing at the top corner of the window. Dad was annoyed: "No German bomber stands any chance of seeing that" he said – "If he can, then he's welcome to try and hit it!" But that was heresy in the ears of the warden; "It's LIGHT isn't it? – GET it COVERED" he shouted, as he stormed off into the night.

Another worry was that the enemy might use poison gas, as they had in the First World War, so we were all issued with gas masks. These were supplied in stout cardboard boxes which, with a string attached for carrying them, served as containers for carrying the masks to and from school. I remember the rather hilarious time we had at school one day, when the class master decided to have a trial lesson with our masks on. The muffled sound of his voice and of our own voices as we tried to answer questions, we thought extremely funny. The experiment was not repeated.

The Evacuation
Of all the preparations for coping with the expected air raids, one of the biggest to organise must have been the 'Evacuation'. This involved the

moving of thousands of school children, plus mothers with children under five, from towns and cities thought to be at risk, to be billeted with people living in relatively safer areas. King's Lynn was to be one of these receiving areas and this must have been rather a personal blow to my parents – after having just settled in and begun to appreciate the extra living space of their new home, they were going to have to share it with strangers.

Eventually, the special train arrived at Lynn with its 'Evacuee' passengers and they were taken to hastily set-up reception centres in the town. Mum took me with her to St. James' School in Hospital Walk, our local reception venue, to meet the new arrivals. My Aunt Doris, the youngest of Mum's three sisters, also went. I remember the lines of children waiting, some on their own and some, the very young ones, with their mothers, whilst the appointed officials busied themselves in recording the visitors and matching and allocating them to their host families.

The family, with whom we became involved, was a mother with a tiny baby and two older boys. The younger of these two was about four and the older one eleven, my own age. The official suggested that Mum should accommodate the mother and baby and that Auntie Doris should have the two boys - which seemed a sensible arrangement. But, of course, things are not always that simple. When the younger brother understood what was proposed, he started to cry and bawled out in no uncertain terms that he was NOT leaving his Mum! Anyway, a solution was worked out which was quite ingenious – and it involved ME! The youngster would stay with his mother and the baby at our house; I would accompany the elder brother and stay with him at Auntie's house. So, with this agreed, I was to become an 'evacuee' in my own town.

I told myself that this arrangement should be quite fun. Aunt Doris, the youngest of Mum's three sisters, was my favourite aunt. Furthermore she and Uncle Len, who had only been married a short while, lived in a smart new house which, I remember hearing on the family grape-vine at the time of their marriage, had cost them £650. The house was a big contrast to the humble rented abodes of the rest of the family. Staying with them was going to be quite a novelty. After everything had been sorted out by the grown-ups I moved, together with Ronald my new evacuee companion, into my Aunt and Uncle's house at 39 Holcombe Avenue.

On the first evening, at bedtime, I discovered that the new house was not yet fully furnished. Until proper beds could be obtained, Ronald and I were to make do with temporary beds made up on the floor of one of the three bedrooms. Uncle Len, who obviously took his new responsibility seriously, stood in the bedroom doorway, I remember, after we were in bed, and reminded us both to say our prayers. Being met with an embarrassed silence, he said: "You don't have to say them out loud." Then he stood there until he received the assurance that they had been said. So began my experience of the 'Evacuation'.

Changes – thick and fast

'Variety is the spice of life', so the saying goes! Changes during this period seemed to be coming thick and fast: Dad had changed jobs; we had moved house; war had broken out; as a consequence of war, the evacuees had arrived, which, in turn, had led to my temporary move to live with Auntie. Also, as I had reached the age of eleven, I was now due for a further change - a move from Junior to Senior school. The school that I was to attend was a brand new building, only recently completed, which lent an added interest to the prospect. Separate schools were provided on the site for boys and girls, each school with its own head – a headmaster for the boys and a headmistress for the girls. The schools were to be known as the 'Gaywood Park' schools. Many years later, in 1989, at a 'Grand Re-union of Original Staff & Pupils' of the school, when I was able to look at photo-copies of the original records, I learned that on the opening of the school on the eleventh of September 1939, 503 girls were admitted and, of the 523 boys admitted, I was admission No.9.

Everything on that first day added to the sense of making a 'new beginning': the newness both of the school buildings and of all its equipment; the fact that I had left behind my junior status and had become a 'senior'; the previously unknown faces of many of my classmates. After we had begun to settle down at our new desks and the class master had introduced himself, partway through the morning we received a visit from the headmaster himself – a Mr Longman. It appeared that he was circulating round each classroom to welcome the boys and to tell us what to expect at our new school.

Mr Longman was a very smart man and looked very impressive but, even in those days, I thought that he looked rather 'old-fashioned'. He wore a black jacket, pinstriped trousers and had a black bow tie. At a guess I would say that, in age, he was well into his fifties. He came over as a very friendly man, but not the sort of man to be trifled with. Seating himself on the class master's table at the front of the class he proceeded to give us a talk, telling us a bit about our forthcoming lessons and of the new school's facilities. He ended, I remember, by giving us advice on how to learn effectively, stressing that this was not just a case of listening. There were more ways than one of getting things into our heads, he emphasised: we would listen, we would read, we would write and we would discuss and, in the practical lessons we would be more active still by doing; all important ways, he said of obtaining knowledge.

The facilities at Gaywood Park, compared with those at my previous school, seemed out of this world. Those that I came to appreciate the most were the well-equipped woodwork and metalwork rooms. I had always liked playing with wood – now I had the chance to learn how to do it properly. We were shown how to plane a piece of wood to size, how to saw, and also whilst I was at the school I began to learn how to make the different joints. I can still see the woodwork master, with saw in hand, demonstrating its correct use; explaining that it only cut on the down-stroke. There was no need to force it into the work, he said, for if it is sharp and correctly set as it should be, the saw would do most of the work.

Another novelty for me was the school canteen and, as I now had further to walk to school, I was allowed to stay to dinner. We were issued with dinner tickets and the cost was 3 pence per day. I don't remember us being given any choice of menu; if anything appeared on the your plate which you didn't like, you just had to put up with it – though this didn't bother me too much as I was not a fussy eater. All the boys of our class who stayed to dinner sat at the same long table with our class master seated at its head. A couple of boys were delegated to collect the filled plates from the canteen counter and place them on the top end of the table, from whence they would be passed along until every boy had received his dinner, whereupon the master would give the word to commence eating.

Life went on; I settled into my new routine and was quite happy at Auntie's. Ronald, my fellow evacuee had been enrolled at Gaywood Park School, so from Monday to Friday we would walk to and from school together, each with our gas mask case slung on our shoulder. At weekends we would both spend time at my home; me to see Mum, Dad and my brother and sister; Ronald to see his Mum, younger brother and the baby.

The month of September came to its end; October and November both came and went and, strangely, the expected German bombing attacks on London and the other cities did not take place – it just was not happening. This period of quiet became known as the 'phoney war'. The effect of this on the evacuees and their families was understandable: many felt that they could just as well have stayed at home instead of having to live with strangers who, in their turn, did not enjoy the inconvenience of sharing their homes with the newcomers. Ronald's mother was no exception: half-way through December she told my mother that she had decided to take her children home and she didn't think that they would be coming back again. So it came about that both Mum and Auntie lost their evacuee visitors, and I was back at home for Christmas.

Some Exciting News
1940 dawned and the 'phoney war' continued; but there were things other than the non-existent bombing to remind people that Britain was in fact at war: such as food rationing and the new identity cards we were all supposed to carry. However, shortly into the new year my brother Geoff,

sister Joan and I briefly forgot all about the war, for we were given some momentous family news: Dad had received promotion at work and we were to move away from King's Lynn. That we were to leave the town of our birth was a big surprise in itself. What made the move thrilling to us, was a further two-fold aspect of the change: firstly, we were going from town to live in the 'country', and, secondly, the move was to the station house of a country railway station – a double excitement: countryside plus trains!

★★★★★

BOY on a BRANCH

Part 2

Introduction

At the beginning of 1940 our family was about to leave King's Lynn in order for Dad to take up his new post, in charge of a country railway station. The station was Wilburton, on the seventeen-and-a-half mile Ely to St. Ives branch line of the London & North Eastern Railway Company. The station house was to be our home over the next four years and most of the incidents described in the following narrative happened as a result of our stay there.

For a general picture of the pre-1940 historical background of the Branch, I am indebted to Peter Paye and his book, *The Ely & St. Ives Railway,* the source of the following quotation:-

> The line had originally opened in 1866 as the Ely, Haddenham & Sutton Railway. An extension of the line to St. Ives was opened in 1878 and the name changed to the Ely & St. Ives Railway. In 1898 the railway was taken over by the main line Company, the Great Eastern, until the early 1920s when the Great Eastern was absorbed by the London & North Eastern Railway.

> Passenger traffic on the line had never been as important as freight. From the end of World War One, when regular local bus services commenced, there seems to have been a continuous decline in the number of passengers carried. A contributory factor was the remoteness of some of the stations from the villages which they served – Wilburton was a mile distant and Stretham a mile-and-a-half. The big decline in passenger services caused the decision by the LNER to withdraw passenger services; this took place in 1931 and in order to further save costs, they closed down the signal-boxes as well.

From that time onwards, apart from some seaside excursion trains, and special trains for fruit-pickers during the fruit season, the Branch concentrated on the conveyance of freight only. Between the two world wars, the volume of freight traffic on the branch had also been affected by increasing competition from road traffic.

A further short quotation describes the situation on the branch very much as it was in early 1940 when my father, Len Marsters, took over at Wilburton station:-

The approach of World War Two brought an increase in materials conveyed to Sutton for forwarding to the RAF airfield at Mepal ... Rationing of petrol also brought the withdrawal of many vans and lorries from local roads and the urgency of foodstuffs meant an increase in freight traffic leaving the branch stations for London and major cities.

CHAPTER 6

Wilburton Station and a Fresh Start

We three children were in a state of great excitement about the approaching move from King's Lynn, to Station House, Wilburton, in the Isle of Ely. I couldn't resist the pleasure of telling my school friends that Dad was to become a stationmaster and that we were actually to live close by the railway. After much impatience the great day came - and we were not disappointed! The contrast between the streets and houses in town, and the wide-open spaces at Wilburton, was tremendous. Our new home was surrounded by fields; the only other dwellings around were four railway cottages a short way along the road to the north of the station.

On arrival we excitedly explored the house and were eager to know which were to be our bedrooms. 'Station House' was in fact a bungalow and, like the rest of the station buildings, was positioned alongside the station platform. Geoff and I were fascinated to find that from the window of the bedroom which we were to share, we looked straight out onto the platform, the surface of which was only a few inches below our windowsill. The trains would therefore pass a mere ten or so feet away from our window, just across the width of the platform. A larger bedroom, which was to be used by Mum and Dad, was also alongside the platform.

The rest of the rooms were on the opposite side of the house, facing south: the bedroom that Joan was to have, a large sitting room and a kitchen. Just outside the kitchen door was a small, enclosed yard. This gave access to a flush toilet on the left-hand side and, on the far side, a wash-house There was no bathroom in the house so we would have to revert to the use of a tin bath, in the wash-house, which Mum regarded as a very backward step, having become used to the convenient bathroom in the house we had just left. Entrance to the property from the public road was gained through a six-foot high solid wooden gate, beneath an archway in the south side of the yard wall and over which a honeysuckle had been trained.

Having inspected the layout of the house and learned which were to be our bedrooms, we sat in the kitchen on various items of make-shift seating to eat the picnic lunch which Mum had packed. Our furniture was still in the railway box-wagon in which it had been transported from Lynn. The wagon was standing in the siding opposite the station platform, awaiting transfer of the furniture into the house. This job would to be carried out shortly by Dad with the help of Mr Hills, the relief man. Mr. Hills had been sent by the Railway Company to run the station after the retirement of the previous Station master.

But we children were not thinking about furniture - we were keen to explore the great outdoors – and asked if we could go outside. After being warned that we were not to interfere with anything, or be a nuisance to Mr Hills, we hurried out of the house and round to the platform. Our only previous experience of railways had been occasional trips on the train from Lynn to the seaside at Hunstanton, during our summer holidays, plus items gleaned from Dad about his job at Lynn. Now, here we stood on the platform of our own station!

We saw Mr Hills watching us from the waiting-room doorway. He was a friendly sort of man, and he asked us our names and what we thought of coming to live at Wilburton. Confirming what Dad had already told us, he said there would be no trains until the afternoon goods arrived at about 5.30pm. When the train came, he warned, we must keep well clear when the loaded wagons were shunted out of the siding. He told us that he was shortly going to help Dad unload our furniture and, pointing to some trees we could see across the goods-yard roadway on the other side of the line, he suggested that a good place for us to play would be in the orchard. 'Mind your ankles as you cross the line' he said.

'Orchard?' we cried excitedly, 'We didn't know there was an orchard!' So, acting on Mr Hill's suggestion, we all trooped down the slope at the end of the platform. We crossed the line, with the level-crossing gates on our left, past the buffer stops at the end of the siding and then across the concrete roadway, which was the entrance from the public road into the goods-yard. On going through a gap in the hedge on the far side, we found ourselves in a grass area with a big cherry tree in the middle. We were ecstatic! What a place to play in! Used as we had been, for most of our lives, to having only a concrete yard behind our house, having now an orchard to play in was going to be tremendous fun.

Moving on beyond the grass we found ourselves in the orchard itself, containing numbers of fruit trees – mainly delicious 'Early River' plums, as we were later to learn. The whole plot, including the lawn area we had first entered, was long and narrow and ran alongside the goods-yard roadway. On the far boundary away from the roadway we made another discovery - a large willow tree. This had obviously been pollarded in the past and now, from the top of its large ten-foot high trunk, there extended upwards a ring of large, evenly spaced straight branches. As we looked up at them, there appeared to be a wonderfully convenient space inside these branches that could be ideal for making a tree-house.

On coming out of the trees at the far end of the orchard and looking across the railway line, we realised that the orchard was about the same length as the station platform. At this end of the orchard we found some interesting looking wooden shedding. There were two doors, the whole being divided into two semi-detached sheds. The left hand one, with a broken down wire run outside and a perch inside, had obviously been used for poultry keeping. This immediately gave us ideas: it would be nice to keep chickens and collect our own eggs - perhaps Dad would get some. Also, there would be plenty of space now for rabbit keeping – another possibility. We really were going to have fun. 'Goodbye to the town - yippee for the country' I thought.

Wilburton Station in the 1940s

As I later learned, during the hey-day of the branch there had been quite a number of staff at Wilburton. In addition to the stationmaster, there had been a porter, an office boy and a signal-man – plus two or three plate-layers based at the station. However, fewer passengers and decreasing amounts of freight carried, had resulted in passenger services being withdrawn completely and a reduced number of freight trains being run. Another economy had been the closure of the branch

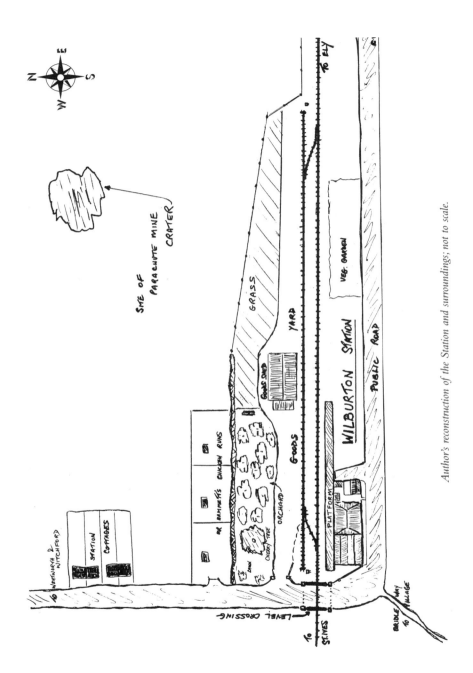

Author's reconstruction of the Station and surroundings; not to scale.

signal-boxes. When Dad arrived at the station only three freight trains per day were being run.

Further economies had been made, by downgrading the position of Stationmaster to that of First-grade Porter; also, the station was to be run single-handedly, except for the help of a seasonal clerk during the busiest period of July to November. Now however, the wartime situation meant that the amount of freight being loaded was rapidly increasing again. With wartime restrictions, any increase in numbers of staff looked very unlikely – so it seemed that Dad was going to have a very busy time. During the summer and autumn months he would be kept quite busy supervising the loading of the wagons in the goods-yard, whilst the temporary clerk dealt with the paperwork in the office.

When we arrived at Wilburton in the early spring of 1940, operation of the branch was very basic. For example, with no signalling to show the whereabouts of the trains, when a train became due, you had to stand on the platform and keep a lookout for it. When the train was seen in the distance you would open the level-crossing gates. Points at the entrances to the goods loop were operated by lockable ground-frames.

The first of the daily trains was the morning milk and parcels train, in the down direction - St. Ives to Ely. This arrived at Wilburton at about 8 am. Next, in the up direction, arriving about 10 am, was the goods train which dropped off into our siding any freight consigned to the station, plus empty goods wagons and vans for the day's loading of produce. In the late afternoon the next 'down' goods would stop to pick up our full wagons which had been loaded during the day, before continuing on to Stretham and Ely. As there was now no passenger traffic on the branch, all the goods trains had a passenger-type guards brake-van next to the engine, instead of a freight type van at the rear of the train, which accommodated the train guard and any milk or parcels conveyed.

The lay-out of the station was a simple one. The single track ran east/west through the station; in the easterly (down) direction towards Ely the next nearest station was Stretham; in the westerly (up) direction towards St.Ives, the next station was Haddenham. Facing points on the track in each direction provided access to a goods loop on the 'down' (north) side, which served a goods shed and the goods yard. There were refuge sidings at both ends of the loop, a short one opposite the station platform at the west end, and a longer one at the east end alongside the goods yard, both refuges ending with a set of buffer-stops.

A large goods shed, standing at the far side of the goods loop just opposite the platform, had large sliding doors on each of the two long sides. The doors on the near-side enabled goods and produce to be transhipped into and out of railway wagons placed alongside it on the goods loop. The doors on the far side allowed similar access for road vehicles on the goods–yard roadway. The shed floor, made of heavy railway sleepers, was constructed at the same height as the railway wagon floors and so it was possible, by using a suitable bridging board, to move easily between shed and wagon when transferring goods from one to the other.

The station buildings, ranged along the south side of the platform, included a small lamp-room containing various lamps and lamp oil, the station house, the office, and two other rooms that, during passenger days had served as waiting rooms. At the side of the office door, which opened into the larger of the two waiting rooms, was a hatch, which had previously been used for issuing passengers' tickets. Outside, near the entrance to the 'Gents' toilet hung 3 red fire buckets. These I believe were filled with sand for dealing with any German incendiary bombs which might possibly be dropped. The public road from Wilburton village approached from an easterly direction, running parallel for about 700 yards on the south side of the railway, turned sharply to the north on reaching the west end of the station and crossed the line over a level-crossing. It then continued on to Wentworth and Haddenham.

The locomotives used on the branch whilst we lived there were known as J15s. I don't remember seeing any type other than this useful little 0-6-0 tender locomotive through the station, although various types had been used on the branch over previous years. The J15 had a total length over the buffers, including the tender, of just over 47 feet.

J15 Locomotive & goods train, typical of those on the branch. Courtesy: Steve Allen.

Wilburton Village School

The first week at Wilburton felt like a holiday. It was exciting living in the station house and being so close to the trains. It was wonderful having lots of space in which to play. We not only had the orchard with the little lawn at one end, but also there was a large area of grass along the north side the goods yard. In addition, alongside the south side of the main track ran a long narrow length of land that had been used by the previous occupants as a vegetable garden. At the end of the week the novelty of the place had by no means worn off. However, we were brought down to earth by a reminder from Mum that she had arranged for us to attend the village school after the week-end.

Monday morning came and we were up bright and early. Getting to school involved a walk along a bridle-way for about a mile-and-a-quarter up to the village. The bridle-way commenced just outside the station, from the bend in the public road where it turned before going over the level crossing. At the end of the bridle-way we continued up the slope of Clarke's Lane to the 'T' junction at the top. Turning left here into the Village High Street we then passed the baker's shop on the right and the post office – a red brick timbered building – on the left. Another general shop was then passed on the right and, just beyond this the end of 'Twenty-pence Road', with Hazel's Grocers shop almost opposite on the left. A short distance further, forking off to the right was School Lane with the school itself standing in the angle between the Lane and the High Street.

The school was run by the Headmaster (nicknamed Nonny) and one other woman teacher and, as far as I can remember there were only two classrooms. The larger of these was a long rectangular room with numerous rows of desks arranged one behind another across the shorter width of the room and facing one of the long walls. On this wall was a series of blackboards and between the wall and the front desks a wide gangway. The groups of desks accommodated two or three different classes, all in the same room and 'Nonny' would move along the front gangway to deal with them in turn. When he was dealing with one class the others would be kept busy with work he had given them to do.

My memory of general lessons at Wilburton is rather vague. I had always enjoyed reading and writing so these presented no problems. As nothing special comes to mind about the maths lessons presumably my arithmetical abilities were up to the standards that 'Nonny' required. The lady teacher, who used the smaller classroom, used to take art lessons, which I much enjoyed. In particular I remember being introduced to the details of making lino-cut pictures – cutting designs in relief with special cutting tools in thick blocks of brown-faced lino, then transferring the patterns to paper with ink or paint which had been applied to the patterns made in the blocks. My most enjoyable sessions were Nonny's gardening lessons, which were quite unique. One of these in particular, at potato planting time, remains a vivid memory – but more of that shortly.

Life in the spring of 1940 was lived against a background of war and 'Nonny' evidently felt it his duty to keep the children informed of its progress, treating it as a part of our education. Things became very desperate for the British Expeditionary Force that had been sent to France and Belgium. Calais had fallen and on the other flank the Belgian forces had been forced to capitulate. The B.E.F. was cut off with its back to the sea and looked like being destroyed by the German army. Mr Churchill, the Prime Minister, warned the country to prepare for 'hard and heavy tidings'. With Nonny's help, we followed the epic story of the seemingly impossible rescue from the beaches of Dunkirk - how the Navy, helped by hundreds of little fishing boats, pleasure boats, ferries, and any craft available, rescued more than 330,000 men. Nearly all the men of the B.E.F. were rescued and brought home.

School Gardening Lesson

On a sunny afternoon, about two weeks into my attendance at the school, 'Nonny' took about nine or ten boys for a gardening lesson. There was no garden actually at the school and, as we set off down the High Street, I wondered where we were going. Turning left into Twentypence Road and walking halfway down the hill, Nonny led us through a gate into a large secluded garden, surrounded by a hedge - his own fruit and vegetable garden.

On looking around I noted fruit trees and bushes, and numerous greens such as sprouts, cabbages and broccoli etc. These however were not to be our sphere of operations. Nonny assembled us at the edge of an area that was clear of crops but covered with small green weeds. Apparently it was potato planting time and this was where they were going in. Unlocking a shed he called two or three boys across to remove from inside about four digging spades, a couple of forks - which, I thought, had very thin tines - and two wheelbarrows, plus a long garden line. After sharing these between us Nonny got us organised.

To my surprise, the first thing he did was to send two boys out of the garden, with a wheelbarrow and the two thin-tined forks and I assumed that they had been allotted a different job elsewhere. Next, after stretching the garden line across the end of the plot he started to dig a spit-wide trench across the plot, placing the removed soil into one of the wheelbarrows as he went. Stopping after a short distance he handed over the job to the boys, who took it in turns to dig. As the wheelbarrow was filled, the spoil was taken to the other end of the plot, where it would be ready in due course for filling in the final trench.

After we had completed digging about half-a-dozen spits across the garden, my earlier curiosity was satisfied, for the boys who had been sent off with the wheelbarrow arrived back with a load of farmyard manure, one boy holding the handles and the other, rather like a trace-horse, pulling from the front on a rope. A further demonstration followed from Nonny who began spreading the manure in the bottom of the last trench just dug, before handing over again to us boys. The seed potatoes were planted directly into the manure for, as Nonny told us, they were greedy feeders and liked plenty of moisture - the manure both fed them and helped to hold moisture at their roots.

The transport boys were now given a rest, being replaced by two others, one of whom was me. We left the garden to fetch more manure whilst others continued to dig another suitable width ready for the next row of planting to take place. I had no idea where we were to collect the manure from but the boy I was paired with had done the job before. The route was back up the road to the High Street, continuing past the school to a farmyard a few hundred yards further on - a walk of at least half a mile, I would guess.

In the yard was a large heap of manure from which we were to fill our barrow. Here I learned the purpose of the forks with the skinny tines: they were muck-forks. Using these we heaped a good load onto the barrow and started off back to the garden, my friend taking the handles and me pulling on the rope. The weight on the barrow handles was quite tiring and my partner asked me to take my turn. Once we reached the downhill slope in Twentypence Road the pull from the front was dispensed with, until we came to the garden gateway where the 'trace-horse' was again required for the pull up into the garden.

By this time we were quite ready to hand over the transport job to another pair of boys. The whole afternoon was quite strenuous but enjoyable. Nonny had the whole session organised as efficiently as a military operation - quite clever really, for he not only taught us boys quite a lot about gardening, but managed to produce most of his own vegetables with a minimum of effort to himself! I feel no resentment about this, for Nonny's tuition was my first real introduction to gardening and my interest has remained to the present day.

CHAPTER 7

Many New Experiences

My attendance at the village school carried on happily in the Spring of 1940 but this was to continue only until the summer holidays. For some reason Mum had decided that I ought to attend a town school and she arranged for me to start at the Needhams School in Ely as from the beginning of the Autumn term. I didn't relish the thought of this change, not because of the five mile cycle ride involved, but simply because I was quite happy in the village. However, as I was not being moved immediately I dismissed the matter from my mind.

Nonny's gardening lessons had their effect and I became anxious to start gardening at home. The strip of garden land alongside the railway line, which had been used by the previous occupants, was now covered in weeds. But one week-end Dad helped me to dig part of this and showed me how and what to sow in it. So I now had a garden of my own and full of enthusiasm as I looked down the line-side, I decided that its possibilities were limitless – I could dig as far down the line as I wished! Such was the eagerness of youth...In reality, I just about managed to double the area which Dad had originally helped me to dig.

Another 'growing' experience was when Geoff and I went sugar-beet singling. One Saturday morning a farmer, who was loading some produce at the station, saw Geoff and asked him if we boys would like to earn some cash by singling his beet. The beet field was not far away, to the side of the bridle-path that led from the station up to the village, so we agreed to have a go. We were met at the field and the job was explained to us. The long rows of sugar-beet plants which stretched across the field had already been 'chopped out' by a man with a hoe, so they now stood in little clumps about nine inches or so apart. Our job was to thin the tiny plants, leaving just one plant from each clump. The rate of pay was four pence a row. We thought it would be quite easy, but we were mistaken: it was rather a fiddly job to thin out the plants and our progress along the rows was much slower that we had expected. Our backs began to ache after a while and the rows of beet seemed almost endless. I think that we did about two rows each before packing up and neither of us volunteered for that job again!

As time went on we acquired quite a number of livestock – some, such as our rabbits and a colourful bantam cockerel, were regarded as pets. Others, like the goat and the hens, were for more utilitarian uses. The cats, I suppose, came under both of these headings for whilst we made quite a fuss of them they were also intended to keep any rat or mouse populations within bounds. One of these cats, a big tabby named 'Fluffy' became Dad's favourite and when he sat down in the evenings the cat would often lay stretched across his shoulders.

One day, however, the cat earned Dad's amused criticism. As Dad had passed by the open door of the goods shed he spotted Fluffy who was lying on some folded sacks on the shed floor. Just then a large rat emerged from a hole in the floor and, seeming not to notice the cat, walked across the floor within a couple of yards of the cat's nose. Fluffy sleepily watched the rat pass until it was out of sight, then calmly closed his eyes as if to go to sleep. Dad joked that it was obviously no use relying on Fluffy to keep the rat population down. He couldn't decide whether the cat was feeling lazy or, as the rat had been quite a large one, whether he had decided that 'discretion was the better part of valour'. However, the incident made no difference between them – Dad and Fluffy remained on extremely friendly terms.

We had been keen to have some poultry and were looking forward to collecting our own eggs, but before he would buy any Dad insisted that the old poultry shed in the orchard needed a good cleaning, so we set to and started on it. We children scraped the dirt from the perches, cleaned out the nest boxes and put in fresh straw, whilst Dad did some repairs to the shed and the attached wire run. When all was ready he obtained some point-of-lay Rhode Island x Light Sussex pullets. Watching through the wire as these handsome birds alternately scratched in the straw of the run and then stepped back to see what they had unearthed, was quite an entertainment – and later, after they began laying, searching in the nest boxes for their eggs was fun.

Our first goat-keeping experience was not so successful. Mr Turner, I think his name was, at Stretham station, bred goats as a sideline and he sold us a big brown goat that had been mated and was thought to be 'in-kid'. We kept her in the shed next to the chicken house and during the daytime when the weather was good used to stake her out, on a long chain, on the area of grass next to the goods-yard. She was quite a strong goat, so the metal peg used to secure the chain was a long heavy one and we used a heavy hammer for knocking it into the ground. When you did this, as we soon found out, you had to keep a weather eye open for 'milady' for she had a habit of trying to butt you in the rear with her horns as you were bending over the stake. We kept her for a couple of months or so, but it became obvious that she was not in kid. Dad discussed this with Mr Turner and he agreed to replace the goat with another one. The replacement was a pretty little horn-less black-and-white goat that was actually in milk. Geoff learned to milk her and thereafter became milker-in-chief, using one of Mum's pudding basins as the receptacle I remember.

Geoff and I were never at a loss for things to do; when we weren't playing games, feeding the livestock, seeing produce being loaded into the wagons or watching them being shunted when the train came to pick them up, we could always play in the tree-house. This was the big willow tree mentioned earlier, with its nice space at the top of the bole within the encircling branches. We had woven a wall of long thin willow shoots around the branches, which gave us a private den on the inside and, with just one space left between two branches for access, and a home-made rope-ladder which could be pulled up we felt unassailable. One of Geoff's favourite occupations when he didn't want to play, was to sit up in the tree-house all on his own and read a book.

Though we children continued to enjoy our new life at our little country station, the wartime situation inevitably affected us. Food was rationed for one thing, and generally there was an air of worried expectancy. Once more we had evacuees to stay - two quite young children, a brother and sister. The British army, having been thrown out of Europe at the beginning of June, was desperately trying to reorganise and re-equip in order to resist the expected German invasion. In an attempt to prepare for this a volunteer defence force, the 'Home Guard', had begun to be organised.

One evening Mother was invited to call to see Mrs. Wade, a neighbour at Hawks Nest Farm just across the field to the west of the station. Geoff and I accompanied her. There we also met her sons, two young men who were members of the Home Guard. During the evening these two showed Geoff and me the rifles and bayonets with which they had been issued. I don't think that they had received any ammunition at this stage, but they took great delight in showing us how the bayonets fitted on the end of the rifles.

The taller of the two took up an appropriate stance and went through the motion of an imaginary stabbing with his rifle and bayonet. As he did so he said with feeling: "If I could get near Mr. Hitler that's what I would cheerfully do to him, and I'd twist it like this before pulling it out again". I have reflected since, that had he had the opportunity to convert this bloodthirsty threat into action, he would possibly have saved millions of people from untold misery and death suffered over the terrible years that were then still ahead.

Another memory of that evening's visit is of the lady of the house showing Mum inside her pantry. It was a sizeable 'walk-in' pantry and, leading us through the door she pointed to two large sacks standing on the floor. They were full of sugar. Food rationing had begun and the amount of sugar allowed was quite meagre, so the lady was very pleased with herself at having been able to stock up to this extent. She made a lot of jam, she told Mum, so the sugar would be very useful; hopefully it would last for the 'duration' (meaning the duration of the war). Alas, we had no idea at the time just how long the 'duration' would prove to be and I imagine that she ran out of sugar long before the end of the war.

Other neighbours who sometimes invited us round were Mr & Mrs

Gillett. The Gillets, who I would guess to be in their fifties, occupied the furthest dwelling of two pairs of semi-detached cottages just down the road to the north of the station. He was a railway platelayer and occasionally he would be seen walking along the track through the station with his long-handled hammer, checking that the wooden blocks, which held the rails in place, were tightly hammered home.

Mr. Gillett had a nightly routine of preparing his kindling wood ready for lighting their living room fire the next morning. Most materials were in short supply at the time and, to help the 'war effort', everyone was careful to avoid waste. During the evening of one of our visits, Mr. Gillett got out his box of previously chopped kindling and showed us his method of preparing it so that he could light his fire without the use of any paper. Using his 'shut-knife' he took each stick of wood in turn and whittled down the sides of it to produce lots of curly slivers of wood which were not cut right off, but retained along the sides of the main stick. The resulting mass of fine slivers would ignite easily when the wood was laid on the fire and a match applied to them, thus avoiding the use of paper, which I thought was quite ingenious.

Mr. Gillett was a cheerful, friendly man and we took quite a liking to him; however, another of his daily routines with which I became acquainted during our visits did not impress me at all! From the introduction of food rationing, with the objective of keeping up his strength, he had taken to the practice of having a cup of hot milk every night before going to bed. "Ugh - how horrible!" I thought.

Mr. and Mrs. Hammett were other neighbours, who also lived in one of the railway cottages. Mr. Hammett used to cycle to work at Haddenham, the next station in the 'up' direction, where he was a clerk. He had made a point of informing Dad that the position he held was that of *Chief* Clerk. The Haddenham station layout was much bigger than ours at Wilburton, but whether there was more than one clerk there, I don't know. For some reason Dad and Mr Hammet never got on very well, always seeming to 'rub each other up the wrong way'; Dad regarded the other man as interfering. I remember in particular Dad telling Mum about one altercation which had taken place with Mr. Hammett on the telephone when the latter had told him how he should be doing something or other at Wilburton. Dad had retorted that he himself was responsible for operations at Wilburton, not Mr. Hammett, whereupon Mr Hammett had replied that he would not be put right by a porter. Dad's response to that - related to Mum afterwards with great satisfaction - was: "At least I'm a First-grade porter - not a Fourth-grade clerk!"

The Hammetts had three children, all girls. The eldest, Angela, tallish and slim, was about seventeen and attended the Girls High School in Ely. Bunty the middle daughter, who would be about two years younger, was much more buxom. The youngest girl of about my age was named Coralie; Mum regarded her, I recall, as being rather precocious. It was some time before it occurred to me that the initial letters of the girls' names were in alphabetical order: Angela, Bunty, and Coralie. It would have been interesting to see what names the Hammetts would have given to any further daughters, if any had arrived.

I remember a Saturday morning when Angela called round to the station and knocked on our kitchen door to speak to Mum about something. She was a very friendly girl and Mum quite liked her. After they had sorted what Angela had come about they continued talking in the kitchen doorway for some minutes. It was a very warm, sunny morning and Angela was wearing a light summer dress. As she stood in the doorway, she had no idea that the bright sunshine behind her had the effect of showing a wonderful silhouette of her attractive figure to the admiring boy sitting inside the kitchen!

Mr. Hammett had a large flock of poultry as a spare-time occupation. These he kept on a long narrow strip of land just beyond the north boundary hedge of our orchard. He had divided the strip with posts and six-foot high wire netting into three separate pens, with a poultry house in each pen Every morning and evening Mr Hammett walked down the road from his nearby cottage, with a metal bucket on each arm, to feed his hens and to collect their eggs. At week-ends, one or more of his daughters would usually do the job for him and we would often see them through the orchard hedge. As I watched them pass from one pen to another scattering corn from their buckets, with the hens gathering expectantly at each succeeding pen gate, I quite envied the girls. I thought how nice it would be, to be able to keep a large flock of poultry like Mr. Hammett's.

Another character who comes to mind was Doctor Fairweather. The doctor was a fairly small man – in his fifties I would guess – who held his surgery at his house in Haddenham, the next village. I later learned that he had been a naval surgeon, which probably explained his very brusque 'no-nonsense' attitude. His terse manner, coupled with my experience in his surgery one day, left me with an impression of him as an intimidating little man!

I was not often unwell, but I remember Mother taking me to see him on this particular occasion. Our turn came to be called into the surgery, and Mum explained that I had been feeling unwell. Turning to me the good doctor said: 'Take your shirt off boy and come over here.' I did as he asked and he examined me with his stethoscope. Then, having decided that he would take a blood test, he said: 'Sit down, boy.' Going to a cupboard he removed what, to me, looked some rather fearsome equipment: a large syringe, some piping and a glass jar. With hardly a pause, he punctured me in the crook of my arm with the syringe and proceeded to transfer blood from me to the jar. Bemused, I sat watching my blood rising in the jar – and started to feel very faint. Instantly a heavy hand fell on the back of my head and propelled my torso downward, with the stern command: 'Put your head between your legs, boy!'

CHAPTER 8

Watching Railway Activities; Admiring the Shunting

After school and at week-ends we children used to amuse ourselves by watching routine activities at the station. In the Spring of 1940, apart from parcels and the tail-end of the previous season's potatoes, there was relatively little freight arriving at the station and, when the potatoes were finished, there was rather a lull for a while. On the receiving side, there would be various farming-related items such as animal feeds; also the 'returnable' fruit containers from the London and other markets for the local growers' use in the forthcoming season. Later, in June and July things began to speed up again with the start of the new season's fruit crops and from then on Dad became quite busy supervising the loading of the crops into the wagons. To make sure that the loading was properly done he would help with much of the loading himself, which meant that life was quite strenuous for him. Another job that had to be attended to was the labelling of the wagons, showing their contents and destinations.

Once the season was getting well under way, Dad had the assistance of a temporary clerk in the station office for the next five or six months to deal with the paperwork, whilst he himself spent most of his time in the goods-yard. The clerk who was sent to Wilburton to carry out the office duties was a young man of about 20 years of age named Arthur Lawes, from Oulton Broad. Arthur at the time was in fact awaiting his call-up into the navy. War-time travelling was, of course, very difficult, so it was arranged that Mum and Dad would give him lodgings with the family.

Arthur was great fun - always ready for a joke - and we children loved having him to stay with us. He had endless stories about the Navy to tell us boys and Geoff was so impressed that he decided that when he grew up he would like to join the Merchant Navy. When Arthur rolled his shirt-sleeves up he would do it very carefully, making sure that he made the folds neat and exactly the same width on both arms. He told us that he was practising getting them the 'regulation two inches wide' ready for when he had to go in the navy.   One Saturday morning, Geoff and I were talking to Arthur in the office. The mid-morning train had arrived and was preparing to shunt some empty wagons into the goods siding. The crossover points for entry into the siding were located just outside the office and we all went out onto the platform to watch proceedings.

The empties were unhitched from the train; the locomotive took them forward over the level crossing, beyond the siding points, and stopped. Dad operated the points by pulling over the levers of the ground frame and the wagons were backed into the siding.   As the guard was unhitching the locomotive ready to come out again, Arthur said to Geoff and me: "Shall I show you how to turn a ha'penny into a penny"?   We realised that he was up to something but didn't know what. But you always went along with Arthur's tricks, so we agreed that we wanted to be shown how to double our money.

Arthur took some coins out of his trouser pocket, selected a half-penny, walked down the slope at the end of the platform and placed the coin on one of the rails just beyond the points. As he came back up onto the platform it suddenly dawned on us what he intended - when the engine came out of the siding it should squash the ha'penny and make it bigger! We stood on the platform and waited, all agog, to see the result. After the locomotive emerged and had backed onto its train, Arthur retrieved the coin and brought it back to show us. The result was not quite what we had expected: the coin was certainly bigger in diameter, but it was now much thinner, the King's head was unrecognisable and the lettering unreadable - it certainly could not be passed off as a penny - but it had been fun!

Produce Loaded

Two of the local growers were the Cropleys and the Everitts. Mr. Fred Cropley, a genial man of about 50, used to deliver produce from his brother Sid's fruit farm by horse and flat four-wheeled wagon. Whether Fred was a partner, or whether he simply worked for Sid, I don't know, but it was always Fred, in his flat cap, who made the deliveries to the station.   I was later to meet Sid when Geoff and I went fruit-picking for him in the summer holidays to earn some pocket money. Sid was much thinner than Fred, appearing rather austere, and by no means as jovial as Fred. He wore a battered trilby hat and seemed to be an habitual chain-smoker of Woodbine cigarettes which, I could not help noticing, had stained his front teeth.

In June and July loads of gooseberries and strawberries would be delivered to the station yard. The gooseberries were contained in circular wicker skeps; the strawberries in oblong 'chip' baskets. On a Saturday morning, I would look out for Mr. Fred Cropley's arrival with a load of fruit and follow him down the yard, hoping to be allowed to help him off-load the containers into the railway wagon. If Dad came down the yard immediately he would usually help with the loading but, if he was busy elsewhere he would give Fred the number of the allocated wagon, so as not to hold him up, and follow on down as soon as he was able. In this case I would jump up onto Fred's lorry and offer to help. He was always willing to be given a hand and I enjoyed feeling useful.

Fruit crops would be loaded into closed container wagons – 'box vans' we called them – which Dad would have previously inspected for cleanliness. He would have swept the wagon out and removed any loose packing straw, which sometimes would have been left from loads elsewhere. The double doors of the van would be hooked back and Fred would draw alongside with his horse to position the lorry as close as possible to the open doorway. This made it easy to step between the wagon and the lorry.

Starting at one end of the wagon, the chip baskets of strawberries were laid end-to-end across the wagon. A second layer was then placed on top of the first, inserting each basket between each pair of adjoining handles of the lower layer. Continuing this procedure, layer upon layer, you ended up with a stack of baskets across the wagon, rising to a point in the middle. A further three rows would then be placed alongside the first one, in a similar manner. Then, in order to make use of the sloping space on either side of the apex, baskets would be placed at right angles to the first lot at the bottom of the slopes, one basket across two rows. This enabled the stack of baskets across the wagon to be built up level to a reasonable height, so making full use of the available space.

The routine of transferring the load from the horse lorry to the box-van was done steadily and systematically. We would take care to pass each other always on the same side to avoid bumping into each other as we carried the chips in. Alternatively, one would stay in the wagon to stack, while the other passed the baskets in. Some hundreds of chip baskets could be fairly rapidly transhipped from one vehicle to the other.

Fruit such as gooseberries, plums or apples would be delivered in the wicker skeps. These were circular baskets, the larger 'bushel' size being about 24 inches in diameter and fourteen inches in height; the smaller sized ones, known as 'strikes', were approximately fifteen inches in diameter and ten or twelve inches high. The weight of the larger ones I found hard work to lift; the smaller ones I could manage quite well. The baskets were of very sturdy construction and, with the fruit filled to just below the rims, could be easily stacked one above another in the wagon.

We had strict instructions from Dad that we were not to help ourselves to any fruit from the containers, as these had all been weighed into set weights prior to despatch. It was impressed upon us that they had to reach the markets still containing full weight, otherwise the senders would receive complaints from the buyers. Most of the wicker skeps were the property of the various market firms and had the name of the owner stencilled on the side. These containers were supplied to the growers for supplying the specific orders of the marketing firms and were known as returnable empties. Apart from paper linings used in the skeps, there was virtually no disposable or throw-away packaging in those days; all the containers had to be accounted for and returned in due course to their owners. Shortages were charged for and would be deducted from the price paid for produce.

Following on after the strawberries and gooseberries would be the plums, and these again would be transported in the sturdy wicker skeps. The plums I remember best were the dark blue, deliciously sweet, Early

Rivers. These would have provided quite a temptation, I think, had it not been for the fact that our little orchard contained a number of trees of this variety, so we had plenty of these juicy items of our own to go at. As the season progressed there were variations in the produce delivered to the station. The Early Rivers plums would be followed by other varieties such as Czars and Victorias and then there would be damsons and various varieties of apples, providing a steady stream of freight throughout the summer.

When harvesting of main-crop potatoes began, a large tonnage would be loaded at the station, all in hessian sacks and weighing one hundred-weight each. A Mr. Everitt used to send a lot of potatoes away; he delivered them to the station in his little motor lorry, which carried about five tons at a time. These sacks were too heavy for me, but Dad, though a quite small man, used to routinely help with their loading. Some years previously he had injured his back in an accident, but as far as he knew, it had completely recovered; we were blissfully unaware that in the not-too-distant future his back was to cause big problems for us all.

Shunting

One of my biggest attractions at the station was to watch the trucks being shunted. In the afternoons, the down goods train from St. Ives would pick up the loaded wagons at each station en route to Ely, arriving at Wilburton at about five o'clock. Using the ground frame and the points at the East end of the siding, the locomotive and a number of wagons would be unhitched from the train at a suitable point and backed into the siding to bring out some of Dad's newly loaded ones for adding to the train. This operation could be repeated a number of times in order to position each wagon at the appropriate position in the train, depending upon its destination.

The hitching and unhitching of the wagons was done with a shunting pole - a sturdy wooden pole of about six feet in length and two inches in diameter, with a curly metal hook at the end. The goods wagons had a large connecting hook and a chain at both ends, thus allowing any wagon to be attached to its neighbour either by its own chain being hooked over the neighbour's hook, or by the neighbouring wagon's chain being hooked over its hook. The end link of the heavy three-link chain would be held with the hook of the shunting pole and the hanging chain would be made to swing backwards and forwards. When enough momentum was gained, the upward swing would be continued and the end link of the chain brought to rest over the large hook of the adjoining wagon.

The Guards made their shunting a fine art. They would often hook the shunting pole onto the front end of a moving wagon and walk alongside it as it approached the wagon to which it was to be attached. As the buffers of the two wagons met and the moving wagon slowed down or stopped, its chain would swing forward and, by means of the pole, he would use this momentum to continue the swing of the chain up and over the hook of the waiting wagon. The skill of this operation was emphasised by the fact that the swinging and connecting of the chain with the shunting pole had to take place beneath the protruding buffers of the wagons.

The goods wagons were designed with a metal frame on each side housing a large brake lever. The lever was operated manually; to apply the brakes the lever was lifted over a securing bar at the top of the frame, pressed down hard between two guide bars and a pin inserted in holes in the bars to keep the lever in position. It was normal practice for wagons standing in the sidings for loading to have their brakes 'on'. Sometimes a wagon would be shunted over the points and left to continue its way into the siding 'free-wheel' fashion, without being attached to the engine. Occasionally the 'shove' could be a little harder than intended. Then, in order to avoid hitting the stationary wagons with unnecessary force, the shunter would use his long shunting pole to gain extra leverage on the brake. Running alongside the wagon, he would drop the brake lever, stick the end of his pole under the frame above the lever and press down hard to bring the moving wagon to a halt. All exciting stuff for a boy of twelve to watch!!

CHAPTER 9

Plum Picking and Bacon Sandwiches

One day during our summer holidays Fred Cropley, who was loading some produce into a wagon in the goods yard, asked Geoff and me whether we wanted to earn some extra pocket money. His brother Sid, he said, needed more fruit pickers in his orchards and would find us a job. We were keen to earn a bit of cash, so Fred told us how to find the orchards, which were located between Wilburton and Stretham villages, and it was arranged that we would go the following day. Next morning Mum packed us up some sandwiches and we rode the couple of miles to the orchards on our bicycles.

On arrival we found that a number of women had already started and were picking plums. They were picking into wicker baskets and using step-ladders to reach the plums; we were given a basket each and told to pick the plums we could reach from the ground. When the baskets were full they were taken across to Sid who was weighing up plums in some of the bushel skeps of the type we had become used to seeing at the station. I don't think that anybody was being paid on piecework, as the pickers' baskets of fruit were not individually weighed, but tipped straight into the skeps that Sid was weighing up.

Our picking was far slower than that of the women, but Geoff and I did our best at it and had both worked up quite an appetite by the time the 'docky' break was announced. The women all went into a shed near the end of the orchard to eat their sandwiches, so we joined them there. Various items were used as seats, mainly upturned skeps with folded coats on top for a bit of extra comfort. Most of the pickers had cheese sandwiches, but when we opened ours we found that Mum had packed us up some bacon sandwiches. On seeing these, one of the women said: "Your Mum is not going to make very much out of you – she's spent more on your sandwiches than you'll earn."

Towards the end of that afternoon, Sid produced a bit of a diversion. He wanted to ensure a certain number of full skeps were achieved before the time came for the pickers to leave off, so he decided that he would shake some ripe plums off one or two of the trees. He spread a big canvas sheet under the first tree. Then, using a long pole that had a metal hook on the end, he placed the hook round a branch near the top of the tree and gave it a vigorous shake. As the plums dropped onto the sheet below a few of them were split, but most landed unharmed, and Sid got us to pick them up into our baskets. This was much quicker than picking them off the trees and when we had finished picking up round the next tree, Sid had achieved the quota of full skeps he had wanted.

At leaving-off time we left the orchard and cycled home. How much we earned and when we were paid I cannot recall – neither do I remember doing any further fruit picking for Sid. Perhaps the lady who had spoken so disparagingly about our bacon sandwiches had been right after all and Mother had decided that fruit picking was a waste of time?

Sunnycroft Farm
Since our arrival at Wilburton station, there had been so many new experiences to absorb us that our model farming toys which we had so often played with at Lynn, had not seen the light of day. Also, now that we were actually living in the countryside with fields and farms around us, it was a different world from the one of imagination. My earlier ambition to be a farmer was becoming even stronger and the urge was given an added boost as we got to know the Bamfords, a farming family at Witchford. Apparently our parents had been acquainted with the Bamfords in earlier years and now that we had moved so near them, a firm friendship began to develop between the two families, with mutual visits taking place to see each other.

During his younger life, Mr Bamford Senior – 'Grandad' – had left his job as a factory foreman in Bradford and had come to Witchford to try his hand at farming. He and his wife, who was now an invalid, lived in a little brick cottage on the Grunty Fen road just south of the village. The farmyard itself, with its cow-shed and other buildings, was a further half-mile to the south on the same road. Adjacent to the buildings stood the timber-framed and asbestos clad bungalow in which lived Grandad's son Charlie, his wife Olive and their two young sons. The bungalow had been built by the Bamfords themselves with their own labour, and had been named 'Sunnycroft' – hence: Sunnycroft Farm. Charlie was now responsible for running the farm, Grandad B. being less active and semi-retired.

The farm was within easy cycling distance – just under three miles from Station House – and Geoff and I often cycled there on a Saturday hoping to be allowed to help with some of the farm jobs. We were always made welcome and some job or other would be found for us to do. Mid-morning, if we were in the vicinity of the bungalow, Olive would call us into the kitchen for a hot drink and a piece of cake each. Olive and Charlie's two sons, David and John, were quite a bit younger than Geoff and me and not yet old enough to help on the farm. I think, therefore, that although we were only novices, Charlie appreciated our help. On our part we were delighted to share a small part of the farm life.

The little dairy-cum-arable farm had a small herd of about half-a-dozen Friesian type dairy cows. One of the jobs that Charlie occasionally gave us to do, was to take the cows out to the public road in front of the farm-yard and to herd them along the roadside verges so as to make use of the free grass feed. We would take a stick each and try to make sure that they kept to the verges and off the road. There used not to be very much traffic along Grunty Fen Road in those days, but if a car or a lorry did come along I would feel a bit apprehensive; but we managed the job without any mishaps.

Another job was to help Charlie get in some green-feed for the cows from a small field at the back of the farmyard. The area had been sown with lucerne, a fodder plant with leaves something like clover but which grew much taller. Charlie would cut a patch with his scythe and we would rake it up and load it into a little two-wheeled trailer which, when full, we pulled round to the cow-shed. The trailer had wooden extensions, made by Charlie, which fitted around the top and which increased its capacity by more than double. This same little trailer was used by Charlie each morning, but without its extensions, to take a churn containing his daily milk output up to the village, where it was left on a stand at the side of the road for collection by the milk lorry. In this case he pulled the trailer to the village behind his bicycle.

Mention of bicycles and trailers reminds me of a routine carried out by old 'Grandad' Bamford. He himself would often potter round the farm-yard doing light jobs, such as cleaning mangolds ready for inclusion in the cattle feeds. Meanwhile 'Grandma' Bamford would spend time in the bungalow at the farm with her daughter-in-law Olive. When it was time for them to go home again, Grandma would be helped into her three-wheeled wicker bath chair, which Grandad would hook up behind his bike and then slowly pedal the short distance up the road to their cottage. When I first saw it, the sight of Grandma tucked up in her blankets in the chair, and her sedate but snail-like progress up the road behind Grandad's bike, it struck me as so comical that I had to make a big effort not to laugh.

In later years the floor of the Bamford's cow-shed was concreted, concrete mangers formed at the front of the cow cubicles, with dung channels behind, and the milking done by machine. When we first used to visit them, the cow-shed had an earth floor littered with straw and the milking was carried out by hand. Charlie used to sit on a three-legged stool for this task and we would stand leaning on the wall of the shed and watch. Charlie, who liked a joke, caught me out more than once; he would suddenly say something like: "Here, look at this" and I, stepping forward to look, would get a jet of milk in the face as he twisted the cow's teat round towards me and squirted.

I had gathered, from conversations overheard, that money had always been tight on the farm and now that there were two families to keep this was even more so. It was clear that the Bamfords were very self-reliant, for as well as building the bungalow, all the farm buildings had been erected by their own labour and any implement repairs would be tackled as far as possible by themselves. They were obviously quite inventive and one of the things I thought quite ingenious was how they ran a little corn-grinding mill. This mill, housed in a lean-to shed behind the cow-shed, was used for grinding things like barley and beans for inclusion in the cows feed. It had no power source of its own, but was driven by a belt from an old car engine which stood alongside it and was bolted onto a heavy wooden stand, which in turn had been concreted into the floor for stability.

An important part of the dairy cows' diet was hay. During one of my visits Charlie said he would show me how to cut some hay from the haystack, which stood in the yard behind the buildings. I didn't understand his comment about 'cutting' the hay. I had read about hay-making: how the grass was dried in the sun and, when ready, carted off the field and stacked. I also knew that the stacks had to be either covered with a sheet or thatched, to keep the hay in good condition. In my ignorance I had imagined that when the hay was required for use, it would simply be a case of taking off the thatch and then taking forkfuls off the top of the stack – in reverse order in which the stack had originally been built.

Charlie took me round to the stack and when I looked at it I could see that it had in fact had a large chunk, of about four feet square, removed out of one corner, reaching about half-way down from the top. The remaining bottom half had a temporary piece of tarpaulin, held on with lumps of wood, over its top, and a ladder stood against the side of it, obviously ready for access when the next feed of hay was needed. Charlie went up the ladder, removed the covering and stepped onto the ledge, and beckoned me to follow him up. He told me to stay on the ladder and watch and he would show me how the hay was cut out. At the back of the ledge, near the cut edges of the stack, a large wide-bladed knife stood wedged upright in the hay, with a big wooden handle across its top.

With the knife still perpendicular, Charlie grasped the handle with both hands thrust it up and down into the hay, slicing his way along the two back sides of the ledge. The handles were offset from the blade so as to avoid scratching the hands on the wall of cut hay behind them. With the view I had from the ladder I could see that, following the initial building of the stack, the hay had settled into a tight compact mass, which could be clearly seen on the surfaces which had been cut by the knife. The whole thing looked as if some pieces had been cut from a giant cake. When Charlie had finished cutting along the edges of the ledge, he asked me to pass him up a fork, which he used to throw down some substantial slabs of the cut hay, prior to taking it in to the cows. On later visits Charlie let me have a go with the hay-knife myself and I became quite adept at it.

Charlie Bamford using tractor and binder in 1949; his sons David and John, now old enough to take an interest. Author.

All Charlie's field work, the ploughing, harrowing, drilling and harvesting, was carried out using his yellow Fordson tractor, which was fuelled by tractor vaporising oil (tvo), a kind of paraffin. In addition to its tvo tank, the tractor had a smaller petrol tank as it had to be started up on petrol and was then switched over to paraffin after a few minutes of warming up. It had to be started manually, using a starting handle at the front. Sometimes the handle would kick back and on one occasion this had broken Charlie's wrist, which had to be encased in plaster for some weeks until it healed, thus putting him behind with his work, I remember.

For Geoff and me, the most glamorous work on the farm was the harvesting of the corn crops, the wheat, barley and oats, which we both loved to help with during summer school holidays. The corn was cut with a reaper-binder, which both cut the corn and tied it up into sheaves. I think the old binder had originally been made to be horse-drawn and had been converted by having a draw-bar fitted for pulling by tractor. It was exciting to follow the binder round the field and to watch it throw out all the tied bundles – or 'sheaves' as they were known - into neat rows.

At busy times of year such as harvest, Charlie used to employ the casual help of a man he referred to as Mr Evry. As soon as a big enough area had been cut with the binder, the three of us, Mr Evry, Geoff and I, would start shocking (or stooking) the sheaves. Working our way along the rows of sheaves we would collect them up from two or three adjacent rows, to make a single row of shocks. A sheaf would be picked up under each arm and, with the butt ends kept about eighteen inches apart, the sheaves would be bumped down onto the ground with the tops leaning inwards so that they supported each other. A further two pairs of sheaves would be similarly stood on each side of the first pair, thus making up a shock of about ten sheaves in total. In some years when there were thistles in the crop, you would need to keep your shirt-sleeves un-rolled to avoid sore arms.

The shocks were built like this in order to let the air circulate round the grain, which needed a further period to dry well, before being carted off the field and stacked in the stack-yard. Leaning the sheaves together with a space between them at the bottom enabled them to stand up quite well and also provided an air passage through from end to end of the shocks, which helped them to dry out more quickly if they should be rained on. The shocks were usually left in the field for about three weeks to allow the grain to become dead ripe, before carting.

Carting of the sheaves was my favourite time during the harvest. Charlie used two trailers for carting: a two-wheeled trailer and a longer four-wheeled one. As some of his land was on the far side of the village and quite a distance from the farm, in order to cut down on the number of journeys backwards and forwards, he would hitch the trailers behind the tractor in tandem. The two-wheeled trailer would be attached to the tractor and the four-wheeler pulled behind that. In this way a considerable number of sheaves could be transported on each journey from field to stack-yard, though at a steady pace in a low gear.

When collecting the sheaves of corn from the fields, the trailers would be pulled between the rows of shocks and, stopping alongside each shock, the sheaves would be forked – 'pitched' -onto the trailers using long two-tined pitch-forks. They were not simply thrown onto the trailer in a heap, but were loaded on quite methodically, with either Charlie or Mr Evry on the trailer for the purpose. Starting at the front, some sheaves would be placed on each side with their thick butt ends protruding slightly over the edge of the trailer. The middle would be filled with sheaves and then, as the layers were systematically built up, the outer sheaves would be 'tied-in' by carefully overlapping sheaves above them. Wooden raves extended upwards at each end of the trailers which supported the sheaves at back and front and, with the careful upright construction along the sides, quite high loads were possible.

When the first trailer had been loaded it would be roped down with a wagon rope, to ensure that no sheaves were dropped on the journey home. The loader would then climb down the rope and prepare to load the second trailer. One of us boys would sit on the tractor and move it between the shocks, which was quite an asset to the men, for otherwise one of them would have had to keep jumping on and off the tractor. After each shock had been transferred onto the trailer, in order to let the driver know he was ready to move to the next one – and, most importantly, to avoid a sudden un-expected move for Grandad up on the load, Charlie would call out: 'How'd Gee'. Geoff and I would take turns at driving the tractor; the one of us who was not driving would give the men a hand to pitch the sheaves onto the trailer.

Pitching was not as simple as it looked; you had to learn the knack of it to do it well. The tines of the pitch-forks were made with a pronounced curve, so in order to lift a sheaf the tines were inserted with the points facing upwards. As the sheaf was lifted towards the trailer, a slight twist of the wrist to turn the tines over would result in the sheaf slipping off the end of the tines with ease, carried by it's own momentum. The higher the load, the more important this was, for if you stood with a sheaf atop your fork at full stretch above your head, with the tines the wrong way, it was virtually impossible to release the sheaf onto the load. With the tines facing the load it was easy and once the knack was acquired the pitching would become a smooth fluid movement, making the work so much less tiring.

Geoff and I would spend quite a bit of our summer holidays helping on the farm, for the sheer pleasure of it. Although, as we were aware, money was short for the Bamfords, Charlie always made sure to send us home with a gift of some sort – a 'bait' as he called it – such as potatoes, eggs or perhaps some beastings.[3] Our interest in the farm continued long after we had eventually left Wilburton to live in Cambridge. In those later years, as Charlie's own sons became old enough to help, the harvesting progressed faster; when carting we were able to load both trailers at the same time, with two loaders and more of us pitching. But all that was then future, so I'll go back to the happenings at Wilburton station.

---

[3] *Beastings was the first milk drawn off the cow after it had calved. Mother would use it as a dessert; cooked with a little sugar it was rather like an egg custard.*

CHAPTER 10

A Forceful Reminder – 'There's a War On'

It was the autumn of 1940; at breakfast one morning, Arthur told us that he had heard a strange noise in the night. He was convinced that something had passed over the house, making a scraping noise on the roof. As nobody else had noticed anything, Mum suggested that the noise he had heard was probably made by our goat, across in the orchard. However, Arthur insisted that the noise he had heard was not made by the goat, and stuck to his opinion that something had scraped the roof. After breakfast he and Dad went outside to have a quick look around the roof. They found no sign of anything that might have explained the mystery, so Arthur's story was temporarily forgotten.

A few weeks later, whilst Dad was helping to load a wagon with potatoes, he happened to glance across the field to the north of the goods yard. In the middle of the field lay some light-coloured object that he had never seen before. Being curious to know what the thing was, as soon as he and the other man had finished loading, they both went across the field to investigate. The object of their curiosity proved to be a large piece of cloth. Walking round it and giving it a tug here and there, they discovered that it was a parachute, some of the strings of which had been pulled down into the muddy ground. Whatever was attached to it was now out of sight, buried in the wet earth. Was it an airman who had made an emergency jump from his plane? Hardly, they decided; even in this wet soil a body could not have sunk and pulled the ends of the parachute cords down into the ground like this – whatever was down there must be something heavy.

Suddenly, the 'penny dropped' and they realised just how reckless their actions of the past few minutes had been! The thing beneath their feet – on the end of the cords and cloth they had just been walking round and tugging at, was most probably one of those deadly parachute mines which were currently being used by the enemy. With their curiosity so rudely satisfied, they couldn't get away from the spot quickly enough and they rushed back to the station as fast as the muddy field would allow! The delivery man left and Dad hurried into the station office.

He told Arthur briefly of his worrying find out in the field and asked him to get the Police for him on the telephone, so that he could report the matter. As Dad put the 'phone down Arthur said triumphantly: "There you are, what did I tell you – I did hear something scrape across the roof that night, and this parachute must have been it!" The police took the matter seriously and before long an officer arrived at the office. After taking note of all Dad could tell him about the find, he went down to the goods yard to take a look for himself, but this time both he and Dad kept at a respectful distance from the parachute.

The police officer agreed that Dad's surmise of a mine was probably correct but he would have to get the military people to confirm this and to take the necessary action. In the meantime, he ordered, Dad was to arrange that no further trains were to run through the station – any vibration, he said, could cause the mine to explode. However, by this time the evening goods train was almost due and there were a number of loaded wagons in the siding awaiting pick-up. Having thought about Arthur's argument, plus the fact that the mine had obviously been in the field for a considerable time for it to have sunk so deeply into the soil, it was clear to Dad that he had been carrying out his shunting every day during this time. Putting these facts to the police officer he managed to get him to agree that he could let the train come and carry out the day's shunting – so long as he did it gently!

Everybody else, the policeman said, must be evacuated from the station immediately and, as the mine was equidistant from the station and the four cottages just down the road, the occupants of these cottages would also have to move out. I don't know where these people were put up; being local people they probably had relations or friends nearby, but for us who were relative newcomers it was not so easy. But arrangements were quickly made for us and we barely had time to pack a few necessities before we were hustled off, to be accommodated in the church hall up in the village. Dad was to follow as soon as the days work was done.

Although he had argued that it would be safe to let the afternoon train come, with the knowledge he now had – that a mine was probably lurking nearby – it was with some trepidation that Dad completed that day's work. The train crew was informed of the worries about the mine and the shunting operation was done as carefully as possible. Once the train had left, the police insisted that all further trains must be cancelled until the mine had been inspected and dealt with. When all the appropriate people had been advised, Dad was instructed to lock the station buildings and to follow us up to the village. Thus began a period of rather anxious waiting, not knowing what the outcome of this strange situation was likely to be. We were given camp beds to sleep on and I think that we spent two or three nights at the church hall.

The police had told us that the military people would probably have to explode the mine where it lay. We had been extremely fortunate that the mine had been a faulty one and had not exploded when it landed. Had it done so it is certain that the four cottages and the station itself would have been devastated and the occupants killed or injured. It was now hoped that the earth in which the mine lay buried would contain the blast sufficiently to protect the nearby buildings; but we couldn't help wondering whether we would have a home to return to after the forthcoming explosion. Mum, in particular, was feeling very edgy about the situation, though I think that it had given us children a feeling of excitement. The novelty of being accommodated in the church hall added to the sense of adventure. Our two little evacuees were, I think, too young to understand or worry about what was going on.

It was strange not knowing what was going on down at the station. We could only imagine that the army personnel were assessing the situation and preparing to explode the mine. Such happenings in 1940 were very much 'hush hush' to avoid damaging morale and we never did hear full details of the operation – though it was rumoured that one soldier lost his life when the explosion took place. After some impatient waiting we were at last informed that we could return home. I remember that it was late in the day, almost dark, when the family trooped down the bridle-way from the village back down to the station, all of us wondering what we would find when we got there.

As we emerged at the far end of the lane we could see the station buildings and the house, but it was too dark to see whether they had sustained any damage. On entering the house and lighting up, some of the rooms looked in a mess as bits of plaster had fallen from the ceilings where the roof had been penetrated by falling debris. The most exciting find was a big gash in the seat of our settee, for when Geoff put his hand in the hole he pulled out a thick piece of shrapnel, about 4 or 5 inches long, which had obviously been part of the mine itself. Having been the finder of this memento Geoff decided he was entitled to own it and he kept it amongst his prized possessions for quite a time.

Next morning, inspection outside revealed damage to quite a number of tiles on the roof that would have to be put right; inside it was obvious that some of the ceilings would need re-plastering. Beyond this, and the need for a good clear-up of all the debris, it was a big relief for my parents to realise that the damage had been relatively superficial - much less than had been anticipated. The cottages down the road all had similar damage to our own.

Fortunately, the surrounding earth had taken the force of most of the blast, thus largely protecting the station buildings and the nearby cottages when the detonation took place. Now that the danger had passed, Geoff and I were eager to take a look at the crater made by the explosion. Before leaving for school on the following morning we walked down the road as far as the field gateway to investigate. We were not disappointed. Earth from the crater was scattered far and wide across the field and we could see from where we stood on the side of the road that the crater was enormous; it looked to us like the mouth of a volcano. We imagined that if it had been possible to put a pair of the nearby semi-detached cottages in the hole, they would have almost disappeared from view.

A few days after the mine explosion, the mother of our two little evacuees had an unfortunate experience whilst on her way to Wilburton to visit the children. After arriving at Ely railway station and finding that the bus times were not very convenient, she managed to hitch a lift in a lorry to Wilburton village. On the way she mentioned to the lorry driver that she was on her way to see us at the station, whereupon he said to her: "Is it still there? – I heard that it had been bombed". This put the poor lady in a terrible panic, of course, and I can only imagine her feelings as she walked the last part of the journey down from the village to the station. When she arrived and learned what had happened she exclaimed that she was sorry that she had ever considered allowing her children to be evacuated - they would have been better off staying with her in London, she said. Mum was unable to persuade her to let them stay and she took them straight back home with her.

Happy Days

As the excitement of the parachute-mine episode subsided, life continued quite happily for me and my brother and sister. They were still at the village school, but from the Autumn term of 1940 I had been attending 'Needhams' school in Ely, a five mile cycle ride away, which I quite enjoyed. Sometimes I would go via what was called 'Pools Road', north of the station, and up through Witchford village. On the road between Witchford and Ely, I would often be passed by square-backed Bedford lorries, loaded with materials, I believe, for constructing the runways of local airfields. My alternative route to school when I so fancied, was to leave the station in an easterly direction to Stretham, the next station along the line and turning right after the level crossing there, to head across to Little Thetford corner and then on up to Ely via the A10

When I had started at 'Needhams' school, the first lesson I encountered was algebra, a subject I had never learned. The master was a Welshman – nicknamed 'Taffy' by the boys - and on learning of my ignorance of the subject he asked whether I would like to have a go at it. I didn't like to refuse, so said yes. By some fluke I did quite well in the first exercise, which 'Taffy' thought was wonderful. However, unfortunately I had to let him down somewhat, for my effort was indeed a fluke and I never did any good at algebra afterwards, or managed to catch up with the rest of the form.

I had always enjoyed singing lessons at school and history was to repeat itself at 'Needhams' for here, as at my earlier junior school, it was the headmaster who took us for singing. Most of the boys enjoyed these lessons and I remember how we used to sing with gusto such songs as 'There was a Jolly Miller', 'Do ye ken John Peel', 'Oh Shanandoer', 'Linden Lea' and many others.

Occasionally the class was taken to the local swimming pool which, I think, was not far from the Ely railway station. I remember going only once – and that memory is not a particularly happy one! I had never had any swimming lessons before, so before getting into the water, I was fitted into a sort of canvas belt. This belt was attached by a cord to a long pole which the master in charge held as he walked round the edge of the pool, giving me support and, at the same time, instructing me how to carry out the 'breast-stroke'. Suddenly, without warning, presumably because he thought that I had got the actions right, he lowered the pole, thus depriving me of any support. I immediately found myself with mouth and nose full of water, which rather made me panic – and showed the master that my swimming action was not quite as good as he had supposed.

When we were at home, so long as we obeyed Dad's orders that we were to keep well clear of operations when any of the trains arrived, we had more or less unlimited freedom to play where we liked; there were innumerable places to play games such as hide-and-seek. By this time too, we had already made a tree-house inside the branches of the willow tree on the boundary of the orchard and it was fun from there to spy over the hedge, when Mr Hammett or his girls came to feed their chickens. I continued to enjoy my vegetable gardening at the side of the line and when it was potato lifting time, I remember, Dad showed me how to make a small potato clamp with straw and earth so that we could keep some of the potatoes for the winter.

We enjoyed our collection of animals: the little black goat, the rabbits, the bantam, the various cats. Also I used to love to stand alongside the chicken wire to watch the dozen Rhode Island Red / White Leghorn hens, which Dad had installed. The way in which they busily scratched away in the straw and then stepped back a couple of paces to see what tasty morsel they had uncovered, I found fascinating. All in all, our lives at the time were idyllic.

An occasional diversion which I used to enjoy was when the railway delivery lorry called to take items from the goods shed for delivery to local farms, for the driver would sometimes offer to take me for a ride with him. On one summer afternoon during the school holidays he called for a load of animal feeds – Silcocks, I think they were – and invited me to go along with him. This day sticks in my mind because of what happened on the return journey. The lorry was loaded up with the bags of feed and we set off up to the village and then on towards Stretham, delivering to one or two farms as we went.

There was a final delivery to a farm out on the Wicken road, after which we turned round and headed back towards Stretham. Just as we were crossing the bridge over the river Cam we met a farm wagon coming towards us and the lorry driver pulled over to the near-side of the road to give the wagon plenty of room. As he did so he slightly mis-judged his position and the near-side lorry wheels ran onto the verge at the side and, before he could regain the road the front wheel on my side bumped heavily over a drainage channel which had been cut into the verge. I was shot up off my seat by the stiffness of the lorry springing and whacked my head on the low roof of the cab, the driver apologising as he pulled back onto the road. I soon recovered from my rude shake-up and it didn't deter me from riding in the lorry again at the next opportunity.

Italian Prisoners-of-War

Just over a year passed by and we had almost forgotten the mine explosion. Towards the end of 1941, before going to school one day Geoff and I noticed a couple of army lorries stop at the side of the road just beyond the railway cottages. As we watched, some soldiers got out, undid the tailgates at the backs of the lorries and about a dozen or so Italian prisoners jumped out. After they had unloaded some wheelbarrows and various tools such as shovels and picks, the prisoners were taken into the field where the explosion had taken place and it was obvious that they had been brought there to fill in the crater. Feeling very curious, but unable to stay because of getting to school, we decided that we would come for another look after school.

As soon as we arrived back home that day we rushed down to the field to see how things were progressing. Some of the prisoners were filling wheelbarrows with earth and tipping it back into the crater, but others were standing around and chatting. Everything seemed very free and easy; in fact, the only soldier around in charge of the men was actually some way across the field chatting to some of them. This seemed very strange to Geoff and me; we had expected things to be much more formal and strict, with the soldier standing guard at the gate. Soon after this the army lorries returned, work stopped and the prisoners were taken off for the night, presumably to a P.O.W. camp somewhere.

On the Saturday morning we walked down the road to the field to see what was going on. The prisoners were there again, with their wheelbarrows and shovels, with just the one British soldier in charge. One of the prisoners, a short little man, happened to be not very far from the gate where we were standing, leisurely loading his barrow with the scattered soil. When he spotted us he left off shovelling and walked towards us. He seemed very friendly and began to try to speak to us, so we went through the gate into the field.

His attempts at English were not at all clear and I'm afraid that we hardly understood a word of it. After repeated attempts he got rather frustrated and, looking at me, he mockingly said: 'You no spikka Inglis?' I understood this bit - and I suddenly felt annoyed! I'd been carefully trying to understand his terrible English, but he now seemed to be saying that there was nothing wrong with his language ability – that the problem was on my side! I think my annoyance must have shown on my face, for with a big grin on his face, he patted me on the shoulder in a friendly fashion to show that he had only been joking.

It was just after this that I spotted something that gave me a shock. The rifle belonging to the soldier who was in charge of the prisoners was leaning against the inside of the gatepost – but the soldier himself was nowhere near; he was across the field, talking to some of the men. My heart almost missed a beat...had he absentmindedly left the gun behind? I hoped it wasn't loaded, and I had visions of the gun being picked up by one of the prisoners, and used, before the soldier could get back to it. The little Italian had followed my glance and evidently understood my look of concern: beckoning me to look, he knelt down on the ground and made some marks in the soil.

I found that he had done a recognisable outline of the British Isles, plus a further outline showing France across the channel. He pointed to the area representing France, then, moved his raised hands to indicate a running motion. Next, returning to his drawing, he circled his finger round and round the British Isles to indicate the sea all the way round, saying as he did so: "No scarper, no scarper" His drawing and his gesticulations proved far more effective than his previous attempts of speaking had been. He managed to make me understand that if his fellow prisoners had been captured over on the continent escape would have been a possibility, but as England was completely surrounded by water, attempts at escape were pointless. Looking across at the gun standing against the post he waved his arms above his head in a gesture of dismissal, then gave me a reassuring hug, as if to banish my fears. From that moment we became the best of friends. The prisoners' visits continued for a number of weeks, during which time the little Italian's English-speaking much improved, making chatting between us much easier.

Most of the prisoners were smokers and, as cigarettes and tobacco were strictly rationed in their camp, they were always on the lookout for chances to obtain more. Some of the men, who had obviously been given access to a supply of osiers, made wicker baskets in their spare time. They would bring along samples of various shapes and sizes to try to obtain orders from the locals. Whether or not they were allowed to actually sell their baskets I'm not sure. In practice they would arrange to barter them for supplies of cigarettes and tobacco. It was in this way that I acquired a very useful bicycle basket for the front of my bike, by obtaining a packet of cigarettes to exchange for the basket.

The prisoners were a happy-go-lucky bunch of men. They were not very energetic – which the soldier in charge seemed to accept, for he never pressured them to work any harder – but gradually the crater began to fill up again. When the hole was about three-quarters full it became clear that the men would not be able to find enough soil to fill it completely and I was quite sorry to think that their daily visits to the site would soon come to an end. The whole episode had been a new experience for me and I had enjoyed the regular attempts at communication with my new-found foreign friend; I had made a point of visiting the field each day after school and felt I had got to know the visitors quite well.

During the prisoners' last week at Wilburton, the little Italian – Berti Baldisserra -who had been so friendly, took from his haversack a tiny book and gave it to me as a memento of our meeting. The book's title was: 'Libro de Preghiera' which of course, being Italian, meant nothing to me, though from a picture inside I gathered that it had some sort of religious content. Though it has remained in my possession all these

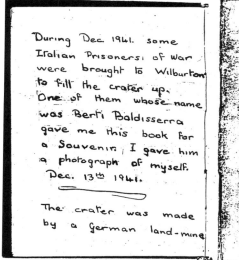

years, it was not until recently when writing these recollections that I got around to consulting an Italian/English dictionary and found that the title means: 'Book of Prayer'. The following is a copy of the inscription, in my boyish hand, which I made inside the book's cover at the time:

Outing to the Cinema

Occasionally, Dad would take Geoff and me on an evening outing to the cinema in Ely and for this we would travel to Ely in the guard's brake-van, on the last train of the day. We would get ready and Dad would change out of his railway uniform before the train was due; when it arrived we would load our bikes into the brake-van so that we could cycle home after the film. Geoff and I thought that it was great to be able to make use of a goods train for our private transport into town! The shunting would be carried out to pick up our loaded wagons and then we would be on our way. It took only about five minutes to reach Stretham, the next station, a further fifteen minutes or so to pick up wagons there, then a run of about ten minutes to reach Ely, the whole trip taking only about half-an-hour from leaving home at Wilburton.

I remember one such trip in particular. The shunting had been done and the little J15 0-6-0 engine started off with the train. Geoff was looking out of the window and Dad and the guard were in conversation with their backs towards me, whilst I stood holding the rim of the brake wheel for support. I knew that the braking of the train was mainly done by the engine driver, so I wondered why the guard needed a brake and, also, how effective it would be. I suppose that it was the fact that I happened to be holding the wheel that prompted the temptation: making sure that both Dad and the Guard were not looking my way, I started to very gently turn the wheel round to see what would happen. After turning it some distance without noting any effect and thinking that if I carried on I was likely to be seen, I gingerly turned the wheel back to its starting point and left it.

On reaching Stretham the guard jumped out to deal with the shunting. Having been convinced that my little braking experiment had not had any effect I had dismissed it from my mind, but was greatly surprised when the driver got down from the foot-plate, walked back to the brake-van and sternly asked which boy had been playing with the brake. On admitting the error of my ways I was told by the driver, in no uncertain terms, that I was not to touch the brake again.

CHAPTER 11

Unwelcome News & Consequences; A Novel Form of Transport

Sadly our childhood was not to continue in such a happy-go-lucky fashion for too much longer! During late autumn of 1941 Dad began having pain in his back and had to pay a visit to see Doctor Fairweather. He advised Dad to take things a little easier, but the nature of the job made this a difficult thing to do and instead of improving his back became worse. The doctor examined him again and arranged for some tests to be done. Shortly after he insisted that Dad stopped working and confined him to bed on suspicion that the problem was serious. The railway company were told of the situation and they arranged to send a relief man to take charge of the station.

Just before Christmas Geoff and I were playing with some plasticine models on our dining table. At the time Geoff was very keen on ships and he had made many plasticine models of the well-known battleships, cruisers and destroyers, plus merchant ships, of the time. These he had carefully made from grey plasticine, using some of Mum's dressmaking pins for the gun barrels, and they looked very realistic. We had just set these out on the table in the form of a wartime convoy, when a knock came at the door, and in walked Doctor Fairweather to see Dad.

The doctor looked at our models and instead of going into the bedroom, stopped in his tracks. He was a very brusque little man and we rather stood in awe of him. He stood for some moments as if in a daydream; then, snapping out of his reverie he pointed to the ships and said: "Who made these?" Wondering whether he was about to be criticised, Geoff said: "I did". "Well done my boy" said the doctor, "excellent, excellent! I recognised those two battleships straightaway, they are the Nelson and the Rodney. I used to serve on the Nelson myself and you've brought a host of memories back to me - capital, capital!" Without further comment he went through the door into the bedroom, while Geoff grinned with pleasure at the doctor's compliment.

But the pleasure was not to last. When he left the bedroom, ignoring us and the model ships, the doctor went straight through to the kitchen to speak to Mum. After some minutes we heard him leave the house. Mum looked very concerned as she went through to the bedroom to speak to Dad and we could tell that the news was not good. Later we learned that the doctor had confirmed the diagnosis as tuberculosis of the spine and that Dad would have to go into hospital for a long course of treatment. Our usual excitement at the approach of Christmas was much overshadowed by this bad news. After Christmas, on the thirtieth of December 1941, Dad was taken into Mansfield Orthopaedic Hospital in Northampton. Perhaps it was just as well that none of us knew then that he would remain there for a full two years before being allowed home again.

The seriousness of Dad's condition had been sprung upon us so suddenly, and events moved so swiftly, that we had little time to adjust to the situation. Christmas came and went and, in no time at all it seemed, Dad had left for hospital in Northampton. We were all left feeling rather shell-shocked and dismayed – not simply because of his absence, but because no-one knew how long it was going to take for him to recover. To make matters worse, we then had a further piece of bad news. Geoff, who had been unwell and under the doctor, was found to have a T.B. gland in his chest and was sent off to Holt Sanatorium in North Norfolk for about seven months of treatment.

Unofficial Crossing Keeper

When Dad had become unable to work the Railway Company had sent a relief man to take over the station. We were pleased to find that he was somebody we knew - Mr. Hills, the man who had been running the station when we had first arrived in the spring of 1940. A few days after Dad's departure, Mr Hills told Mum that owing to war-time transport problems he was having difficulty in getting to work in the mornings from his home in St. Ives. Now St Ives of course was where our first train of the day, the milk and parcels train, started from. If it were not for the necessity for him to be at Wilburton at 8 am to open the level-crossing gates for the train, he would have been able to actually travel to work on the train. He suggested that if Mum would allow me to open the gates for him, this would solve his problem.

Mum was very hesitant about consenting to this unofficial arrangement. I, of course, was dead keen. I reminded her that I had often opened the gates for Dad (though I omitted to mention that this had never been without his supervision), so I could easily do it for Mr Hills, I said. So, with a bit of persuasion – not to say, badgering – from me, she eventually relented and agreed. Mr.Hills was very pleased that his problem was resolved and, for my part, I was highly delighted that under our arrangement he would give me two shillings a week for helping him.

As signalling on the branch had been abolished back in the 1930s, control of the level-crossing gates was now very basic. There was no longer any advance warning when a train left the next station; you simply stood on the platform a short while before the train was due and looked along the line for the first signs of the advancing locomotive. I had often stood with Dad at the western end of the platform close to the crossing gates, looking for the approach from Haddenham of the last train of the day. Some distance down the line was a belt of trees round which the line curved slightly to the left and disappeared from sight. When you saw the locomotive's smoke above the trees you knew that you had plenty of time to walk down the end of the platform and open the gates.

I had no qualms about the job – having often opened the gates under Dad's supervision, I welcomed the chance to do it on my own and felt quite important with my new responsibilities. So, from then on, full of enthusiasm, I got up early and went out onto the platform each morning to open the gates. A number of weeks passed and all went well. Mr. Hills kept his side of the bargain, regularly giving me the promised two-shilling piece each Saturday morning, until I began to feel quite rich.

But one morning, things did not go quite as expected. It was quite misty outside as I left the house and walked round to the end of the platform. I stood for a few minutes looking intently down the line towards the belt of trees from the end of which the train would presently emerge. As I looked, the trees became less and less distinct and it dawned upon me that the mist was thickening into a fog. I suddenly realised just how little of the line ahead I could now see and it struck me with alarm that delay could prove costly; 'No use looking – open the gates NOW' I told myself.

Wilburton level-crossing gates, ground-frame and the siding buffer stops, taken from the platform in 1940; note the shunting pole leaning against the leg of the buffers. Photo: L.W. Marsters.

Hurrying down the platform to the near-side gate I pulled back the bolt, pushed the gate across the line and re-engaged the bolt in the far-side post. My hand was on the bolt of the far-side gate – when I *heard* it! – an ominous clanking suddenly replaced the silence of the fog. Then, I could *see* it! My heart almost stood still as I saw the spitting, clanking monster coming towards me! I felt trapped, penned as I was in the corner between two high gates with the monster almost on me. My instinct was to turn and run back away from the train. but the reality of the situation seemed instantly to flash upon my brain: if I left the gate and ran and ran back I would probably be hit by the heavy timbers of the gate as the train smashed them, even if the train itself should miss me. Terror galvanised the body into action: slamming back the bolt, I hurled the gate across the line with a strength I didn't know I possessed and myself after it. Only just in time! Leaning hard on the gate as it rebounded off the far post, I leant there holding my breath with fear and excitement as the train rumbled past.

The train came to a stop in the station. I stood at the line-side alongside the train, on the far-side from the platform, feeling quite shaken – knowing how narrow an escape I'd had. The gates could not yet be put back across the line as the train had not quite cleared the crossing. However, as the train was a short one, I walked round the end wagon and started towards the end slope of the platform, intending to watch the usual activity on the platform until the train left. Before I had reached the top of the slope the driver, who had jumped down from his engine, came rushing back along the platform to find me. He looked shocked and ashen faced and, on seeing me, he let out a heartfelt cry of "Thank goodness you're all right!" He said that he had seen the gates open just in front of him and been convinced that I must have been hit as I passed in front of the engine; he had rushed back, fearing the worst.

Mr. Hills, on stepping out of the brake van, and seeing the driver rushing back along the train had followed him to see what the trouble was. When he understood from the driver what had happened he too looked quite worried. By now, with the resilience of youth, I had recovered from my shock and was making light of the matter; but then Mother appeared on the scene. From in the house she had an inkling that things outside were not going quite as normal that morning and she came to see what was wrong. When Mum learned of my narrow escape she was livid, I remember, and poor Mr. Hills got quite a scolding from her. She had never been happy about me looking after the gates in the first place, she reminded him; in future he had better make arrangements to be here so that he could open the gates himself. She was adamant that she would not allow me to do it for him any longer!

As far as I was concerned on that foggy morning, it was a case of 'All's well that ends well' and it certainly made a good story to tell my friends at school that day. Just how Mr. Hills managed to get to Wilburton from then on I'm not sure, but get there he did – and I was relieved forthwith of my unofficial level-crossing duties. In fact, Mum threatened me with dire punishments if I ever opened those gates for a train again. My biggest regret was the loss of my weekly two-shilling piece; having a bit of spare cash in my pocket had been a very pleasant experience. I had made use of the cash by paying visits to an Ely book-shop and buying one or two books on country and farming subjects. On looking back on my unauthorised level-crossing episode, I am sure that had the railway authorities known about it, they would not have been very pleased. That then is the story of my brief spell of unofficial crossing-keeping duties at the grand old age of thirteen-and-three-quarter years.

Transport of Delight

Mr. Gillett, the platelayer, would sometimes be seen walking along the line with his hammer, checking the tightness of the wooden blocks at the sides of the rails. But one day I saw him pass through the station on a much more novel form of transport than the usual 'Shanks's Pony'. I was crossing over the rails to go into our orchard when I saw in the distance something approaching from the Ely direction. It was not a train and I wondered what it could be. As it came nearer I saw that it was a little trolley and riding on it was Mr. Gillett with two other workmen.

The thing about the trolley that fired my imagination was its method of propulsion: it had no engine but was powered by a lever, pivoted on a central frame, with handles fore and aft. The men were standing on the trolley platform, two on one side and one on the other, each with one hand on the lever and leisurely pumping it up and down. Looking on with envy I thought how great it must be to dash along the track at ten or so miles an hour on this hand-propelled chariot. Quite unexpectedly my chance came the very next day!

At the time, with Geoff away in Holt Sanatorium, I had taken over the milking of our little black-and-white goat, which had previously been

Geoff's job. It was early evening; I had just finished feeding and milking the goat and was scouting around to find some extra greenfood for her. I had noticed that along the line-side in the Haddenham direction a trimmed blackthorn hedge was now shooting all along its top with lots of soft young growths. I slipped through the level-crossing gates and went down the line to collect a bundle of these new shoots to give to the goat. On returning to the gates, I saw something that I had failed to spot on the way out: there, at the side of the track near the crossing was the platelayers' trolley!

The trolley was parked on a short length of rail at right-angles to the main track. The rail was obviously placed there for such use: it sloped down slightly so that the trolley could not run back and foul the main track and it had a cross-piece across the other end to stop the trolley wheels running off at the back. Situated as it was, on the far side of the crossing away from the station, I had never noticed this little parking rail before. As Mr. Gillett was currently using the trolley, he had obviously left it there at the end of the day ready for use again the next morning. What a find - I could hardly believe my luck! The last train of the day had been through some time ago; now everything was quiet and there was nobody about. It appeared that the coveted ride was within my grasp...and the temptation was irresistible!

After quickly taking the hedge trimmings to the goat I hurried excitedly back to the trolley. I pushed it towards the main track until the front wheels dropped down over the near rail; then with an effort I managed to push it across the ballast towards the far rail. For a while I was stuck with it across the track - I hadn't expected it to be quite so heavy. For a couple of men to manhandle it was easy, but for a boy on his own it was not quite so simple. Before I could have my ride I had to turn the trolley round to face along the track and then get the small flanged wheels up on the rails. With a lot of effort I managed gradually to slew it round until it faced in the right direction – though still not on the rails. But having got this far I did not intend to be beaten. Using a long piece of wood as a lever, I got the wheels up onto the track - and was at last ready for the 'Off'!

I jumped onto the trolley platform and pushed down hard on the rear handle. Nothing happened. The gearing was so high that however hard I pressed on the handle I couldn't get it to move. Realising that I had been able to push the trolley off its parking rails fairly easily, I jumped down again and started to push it from behind. It moved easily; the handles started waving up and down, driven by the now moving wheels and very soon I had picked up a decent speed. Success at last!

Scrambling up onto the platform I grabbed the rear handle and worked it as hard as I could to keep up the momentum. I was delighted to find that having got the thing moving it was now fairly easy. With some energetic work on the handle I achieved even greater speed and I trundled down the line as happy as a sand-boy. After reaching the slight left-hand bend and the start of the belt of trees alongside Hawk's Nest Farm and thinking that I had better not go too far towards the next station, I let the trolley slow down and gradually came to a stop.

Running round to the other end I repeated the 'running start' and was soon hurtling back again with the wheels rattling along the track and sounding like a miniature train. In my enthusiasm I misjudged my stopping distance as I approached the crossing gates. Propelling the vehicle along had been simple enough but I found that trying to stop the handles from moving up and down and to use them as a brake was not easy. At the last minute I had to stop the trolley by jumping off and pulling it hard back to avoid hitting the gates.

If my activities had received no interruption I think that I would have happily continued my riding up and down the line until it became dark – or until Mother came to find me to say it was bedtime – but no such luck! I had just managed my second outward trip and was on the way back towards the crossing when I looked up and saw Mr. Hammett on the public road. He approached the crossing, unbolted the gate and came through – and my feeling of elation suddenly vanished. In my excitement I had overlooked his evening routine of collecting his eggs from the

nearby poultry houses. Now he stood waiting for me as I approached him on the trolley!

Having set down his two egg buckets near the gatepost, Mr. Hammett folded his arms and stood with a very purposeful looking face as he waited to confront me. Looking at his intimidating posture as I came to a stop, I felt very uncomfortable. 'And just what do you think you are doing, young man?' he asked. 'Just having a ride, Mr. Hammett' I replied. 'You should know better' he barked. 'You know you shouldn't interfere with railway property - you'll get yourself into big trouble if you are not careful young fellow. I think that I ought to have a word with your mother'.

I humbly apologised and promised that I would not interfere with the trolley any more. Mr. Hammett helped me to manoeuvre the trolley back into its parking place; then, after reinforcing his warnings with further threats of unpleasant consequences if I ignored them, to my relief, he took himself homewards and left me to do likewise. As I never heard any more about the matter I assumed that he did not say anything about it to Mum. Next day the trolley disappeared and I never saw it again.

CHAPTER 12

A Visit to Lynn goes with a Bang; Novice Signal-Box-Boy

Going back for a moment to 1939, in the June of that year Grandad, who had reached the age of sixty-five, retired from work. After we had left Lynn in the early spring of '40 he was then, of course, no longer able to have such close contact with our family and he decided to accept an invitation to move to live with his other son, Claud, Dad's younger brother. Claud lived at Headington on the outskirts of Oxford and was an employee of Morris's, the motor manufacturers. This move of Grandad's was no doubt a good one, for it meant that he would not be lonely in his retirement, as he might well have been if he had stayed on at Wootton.

In the Spring of '42, very shortly after Dad had been admitted to hospital, Grandad came to visit us at Wilburton for a few days. When he left, he took my sister Joan back with him to Oxford where she was to stay for a while with Uncle Claude, Aunt Dorothy and our cousin Alma. With Dad in hospital and Geoff in Holt Sanatorium, this left only Mum and myself at home and I felt quite the 'man of the house'. It was a difficult time for us all, especially for Mum, as with Dad off work money was very short and had to be tightly managed. Fortunately, fuel for our kitchen fire was no problem, for coal had been a perk of the job with locomotive firemen frequently dropping off lumps of coal for us, and this continued after Dad had gone into hospital.

My experiences and responsibilities during those rather dark days had, in some ways matured me beyond my years, I think. In other ways of course I was still an immature youngster – as witness the plate-layers' trolley incident. I was acutely regretting Dad's absence and also missing my brother and sister. It was fortunate for me that I had plenty of things to keep me occupied, otherwise the situation could have felt much worse. In that spring of 1942, in my fourteenth year, knowing that when I reached fourteen it would be time to start work, my thoughts turned to the question of what kind of job I would get. I had grown up with the idea of going into agriculture and, since we had been at Wilburton that desire had strengthened, so I decided that I would like to obtain a job on a local farm.

I had vaguely mentioned this idea to Mum in the past and had gathered that she was quite opposed to it. Prior to coming to Wilburton, Mum had always lived in the town and I don't think that she had ever come to terms with living out in the country. Whether this had affected her attitude to my wanting to be a farm labourer, I don't know. Alternatively she may have been thinking back to Dad's experience when he was young: before they were married he had left the farm where he worked to go on the railway, which immediately doubled his weekly pay from fifteen to thirty shillings. Anyway, Mum made it clear that she was strongly against farm-work for me and suggested that she would approach the LNER for a job for me on the railway. I was disappointed, but as my enthusiasm for railways was also quite strong, I decided that this would be an acceptable alternative.

A few weeks before my birthday in the May of 1942, I was sick and off school for about a week. On my recovery I told Mum that I thought it would not be worthwhile going to school again, with my birthday so near. My arguments were unsuccessful and she persuaded me to go back and, in fact, I found that I was expected to remain at school until the end of the summer term. As things turned out, it was just as well that I didn't obtain a job immediately after my birthday, for another twist of fate would have caused an inconvenient interruption.

Mum in Lynn Hospital

This circumstance was the fact that early in the June, Mum was taken into the hospital at King's Lynn to have an operation. I had not realised beforehand that there was anything wrong with her, and I never did learn what the operation was for. Obviously, as Dad was in hospital in Northampton, Geoff in the Sanatorium at Holt, and Joan away at Oxford, if I stayed on at Wilburton the couple of weeks that Mum was to be away, I would be on my own. It was therefore arranged for me to stay with Mum's sister, my Aunt Gladys, and her husband Ernest – Uncle 'Nick' -

in their home in Kepple Street.

Auntie's house was very near the Lynn hospital so it would be easy for me to visit Mum. Another thing that pleased me: I was able to skip school for a couple of weeks. Apart from being lectured by Uncle Ernest as to what I could and could not do, I was given quite a bit of freedom, so each day I was able to amuse myself by visiting some of my old Lynn haunts. Aunt and Uncle had no children of their own and, as both of them worked full-time in town, neither of them would have been available for me during the day in any case. It was arranged for me to have my mid-day meal by calling in at Lowe's Restaurant in Norfolk Street where Auntie was Manageress.

The taking of restaurant meals had never been a practice indulged in by my family; even had they wished to, lack of money would have prevented it. It was therefore quite a new experience for me to have all my week-day lunches at Lowes during the two or three weeks Mum remained in hospital. Auntie used to sit me at a little table on my own and whilst waiting to be served by one of the waitresses I could look around and observe what was going on around. I knew nothing, of course, about 'menus' and that normally one would have a choice of which meal was ordered in a restaurant. It came as no surprise, therefore, when the meat and veg. course was simply put before me without any choice being offered and, later, the sweet arriving in the same way. Obviously Auntie had decided what I was to be given.

Each day, just after one o'clock I think it would be, a number of gentlemen started arriving at the restaurant. From the various comments as they came in it soon became obvious that they were 'regulars' and were well known to the waitresses, who sat most of them together at one of the larger tables. It was clear that the men were employees from local shops in the town who habitually came to Lowes for their mid-day lunches. Amongst them was Uncle Ernest – or Uncle 'Nick', as we had always been in the habit of calling him – his surname being Nicholson. Uncle Nick was a watchmaker who was employed by the well-known watchmakers and jewellers, Burlinghams, in the High Street. There would be quite chatter from this table as they talked 'shop', plus a lot of banter and hilarity and it was quite an entertainment for me to listen to them.

One Friday evening, Auntie and Uncle decided to take me to the cinema in the town. After the film we walked back to Kepple Street and we had barely entered the house, when there was a terrific explosion. The bang was so loud that it seemed that it must be extremely close-by. After a very few seconds there followed another similar explosion, upon which Uncle Ernest, realising what was happening, jumped into action. Auntie and I found ourselves grabbed unceremoniously and quickly hauled into the cupboard under the stairs. The cupboard was used as Auntie's pantry and we all stood, squeezed together in the tiny space between the shelves of foodstuffs. Uncle had hardly time to pull the door to behind us before there followed a third, and then a fourth loud explosion.

The bombs had taken us completely by surprise; none of us had heard a prior air-raid warning being sounded; maybe it had been given whilst we were in the cinema and we were not aware of it. It is also possible, of course, that there was no warning because the single enemy plane had not been detected. I think that it must have been fairly soon after this that Mum was discharged from hospital and we returned home. I did not manage to find out at the time as to exactly where the bombs had fallen. It was not until some years later that I learnt that the last of those four bombs had destroyed the Eagle Hotel in Norfolk Street with great loss of life. It was with shock that I learnt too, that the father and elder brother of my Kirby Street playmate, Peter Adams, were amongst those killed in the hotel.

Starting Work

Mum's approach to the Railway Company was successful and the L.N.E.R. agreed to give me a job. I have a vague recollection of having a medical examination, before starting work, though I have no memory of where it took place. This would have been not only to check my physical fitness, but also to confirm that other very important requirement for a railway employee, that I did not suffer from colour-blindness. I obviously passed the examination, for I was accepted to fill a vacancy in the signal-box at Ely North Junction, as a 'box-boy'. My wage was to be one pound two shillings and sixpence for a six-day forty-eight-hour week.

Before starting the job I was issued with an L.N.E.R. uniform. This consisted of: a pair of trousers, a long-sleeved waistcoat with lots of small metal buttons, each bearing the LNER initials, a jacket with three larger LNER buttons, and a peaked cap which had an LNER badge pinned on the front. Donning my uniform and surveying myself in the mirror I thought that I looked quite impressive and could hardly wait for the day when I would wear it officially for the first time. I was given a starting date and, with all the arrangements now made I began to look forward to starting my working life. The prospect of working on the main-line, I decided, would be much more exciting than the three-train-a-day set-up I had been used to on the branch station at Wilburton. Ely North Junction signal-box was located about 2 miles to the north of Ely station – about a 7 mile cycle ride from home.

The great day came at last and I felt quite grown-up knowing that I was about to begin earning my living, though I did have some 'butterflies' in my stomach. In spite of my occasional impetuous boyish escapades, I was not a very self-confident or assertive boy, but rather quite diffident. My first weekly shift was to be the 2pm 'till 10pm late shift and, having had all morning to think about it, I began to have some misgivings. Not knowing quite what to expect, I wondered whether I would cope with what the job required of me. After Mum and I had eaten our mid-day meal I put on my new uniform and, not wishing to arrive late, I got out my bike and left home well early to cycle to work.

After cycling through Ely I took the Queen Adelaide road, looking out as I went for a pathway on the right-hand side which, I had been told, would lead me to the railway line. Taking this path down to an unmanned set of gates I crossed the line, turned left and continued for some distance down the side of the line, which brought me to the junction and the signal-box itself. The directions I had been given had proved easy to follow and I had arrived about fifteen minutes early. I was later to learn that arrival at the box 10 minutes early was quite a normal practice and was, in fact, something expected.

I placed my bicycle against the rear wall of the signal-box and, with the 'butterflies' more active than ever, was starting towards the wooden staircase at the far end, when another cyclist arrived and placed his bike alongside mine. Looking at my new uniform he realised that I was the new box-boy and shaking hands, he introduced himself as Jack Haynes. He was the afternoon signal-man with whom I was to spend my first shift. To my relief he seemed a very cheerful and friendly man and instinctively I felt that I would get on well with him - which had the effect of calming somewhat my fluttering stomach as we walked up the stairs and into the box.

Jack's arrival, and my favourable impression of him, were quite fortunate for me. If I'd had to enter the box on my own, my impressions would have been quite different, for Fred Hallam, the signal-man whose shift was about to end, was a very different kind of man. As we entered, Fred, who was a short thickset little man, stood facing the row of levers ranged along the left-hand side of the box. With one hand resting on the top of a lever, he was listening intently to a bell that was clanging in front of him.

When the bell stopped he responded with some very quick staccato raps, rather like Morse code, on an instrument above the levers. Then, he looked sideways at us, greeted his colleague Jack Haynes and, with a very quizzical look, asked me if I was the new box-boy. The way he held his head, with a searching and inquisitorial sort of stare beneath his bushy eyebrows, made him seem so dour and severe, I got the impression that whatever answer you gave to his questions would be bound to be wrong! I felt very uneasy under his gaze and was glad that I was not starting work with him that afternoon.

I was pleased when Jack Haynes released me from Fred's overpowering gaze by introducing me to the box-boy, who was standing at a tall desk on the right-hand side further down the box. Looking at this lad I realised that I knew him; he was Jim Hooker, slightly older than me, and he too had been a pupil at Ely Needhams and had left school the previous year. Seeing him here was quite a surprise. I had been by no means exceptional at school; in contrast Jim had been brilliant, the most outstanding boy in the school. He had been held up to us lesser mortals as the ideal example of effort, brains and achievement. Suddenly, realising that I was starting work on the same job that Jim Hooker was doing, I had another attack of self-doubt.

Jim explained to me very briefly what his duties were and told me, in a whisper that Jack Haynes was a very good chap to work with and that I would get on well with him. Meanwhile Fred was briefing Jack on the current traffic situation before actually handing over duties and leaving for home. Jim went home too and I was left to start my duties under the tuition of Mr. Jack Haynes. To my relief, I found that Jim's opinion of Jack, and my own first impressions of him when I had met him outside the box, were more than confirmed. He really was a great chap to work with; he was cheerful, he liked a joke, and as far as tuition was concerned he was helpful and patient.

Novice Signal Box Boy
Soon after the early shift staff had left for home, quite suddenly, it seemed to me that all hell was let loose: first one bell rang, then another – and yet another! On the first ring of a bell – a single ring whose purpose it seemed was to call his attention – Jack would respond by a single rap of his own. The bell then would break out into a number of staccato rings in quick succession. He would reply to this seeming cacophony by repeating the sequence of the rings on the answering instrument. At one point, confusing me still further, Jack responded to two bells at once and stood there listening, with apparent ease, to the messages pealed out by two bells at once! In between all this he would dash to the tall desk at the side of the box, consult the large clock which hung above it, and make a number of entries in a big book on the desk before dashing back to pull various levers across the frame.

Watching all this intense activity I stood helplessly by, feeling thoroughly bewildered and useless. Evidently realising from the look on my face how

I felt, Jack told me not to worry and said that I would take to it all like a duck to water. Though I didn't say so, at that moment I was not convinced! After all the activity on the various bells there followed a great deal of activity outside the box: trains passed the box in quick succession and disappeared in all directions. Jack instructed me to look out of the window as each train approached and to check that it had a tail-lamp attached to the rear of the last coach or wagon - he emphasised that I must be absolutely certain about this, as it was most important.

At last, here was something that I could do, which made me feel happier and less like a 'spare part'. It was exciting too to watch the big main-line locomotives as they approached and then thundered past, with their trains rattling over the points - much more interesting than the little J15 locos. I was used to seeing at our little branch station at Wilburton! Later, as things quietened down somewhat I asked Jack why it was important that every train should have a tail-lamp attached. He told me that it was not unknown for a coupling to fail and for a train to become divided. A tail-lamp at the end of the train was confirmation that the train was complete. The sighting of the lamp as the train passed by the box therefore meant that you could be certain that the whole of the train had gone past and that it had not left part of itself behind somewhere. That was why it was important to *see* it!!

Before he had left for home, Jim Hooker had explained to me that my main job would be to record in the train register all the coded messages that were given, and received, on the different bells. Whilst all the frantic activity just described was going on, it was the signal-man himself who, of necessity, was doing everything. I began to think that if things continued like this then he would never have chance to teach me my job. However, once the three or four trains had passed   - and I had successfully spotted all their tail-lamps and reported on them to Jack   - things quietened down a little and he started to explain things to me.

Fixed above the row of about seventy-five levers, was what was referred to as the 'Diagram'. This was a large frame, of about five or six feet in length and three feet wide, covered in glass and looking like a huge

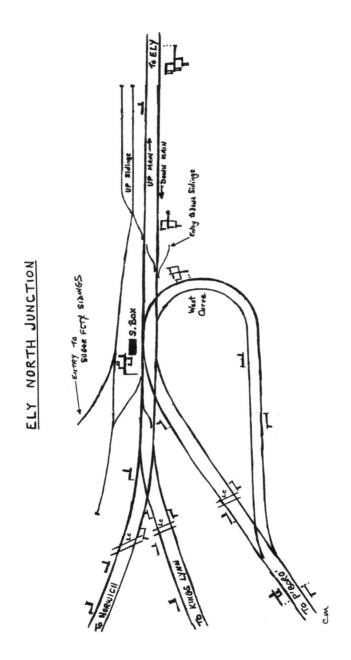

ELY NORTH JUNCTION

To ELY

UP Sidings

UP MAIN

DOWN MAIN

Entry to Down Sidings

West Curve

ENTRY TO SUGAR FCTY SIDINGS

S. Box

TO NORWICH

KINGS LYNN

TO P'BORO'

C.M.

A reconstruction, from the Author's memory, of the Junction lay-out as it was in 1942/43. (Down sidings omitted) picture-frame. Beneath the glass was a plan of the whole layout of the junction and, pointing up at it, Jack explained the layout to me. All the routes through the junction were of double track, one being the 'UP' line and the other the 'Down' line.

The near-side track which ran immediately below the front of the signal-box, was the 'UP' line on which trains passed us heading south for Ely Station and from thence on 'UP' to London. The far-side track was the 'DOWN' line on which trains passed to our north. Just past the box, this 'down' line divided into three separate directions. First it branched to the left in a north-westerly direction and became the Peterborough line. Next it branched right to the north-east and became the Norwich line. The middle line of the three, to the north, was the King's Lynn line.

In addition to this basic layout, just beyond the south end of the box the tracks branched off to the right (west), curved right round upon themselves until they were running north-west and then joined the Peterborough' line in the 'down' direction. This piece of track was known as the 'West Curve'. It enabled 'up' trains off the Lynn or the Norwich line to be routed round the curve and then 'down' onto the Peterborough' line, and vice-versa, without having to travel up to Ely station and then come back down again.

A striking feature of the 'diagram' was the incorporation of lights at numerous points along the tracks. When a train passed over a section of track represented by a light the light would go out thus informing the signal-man exactly where the train was. Also shown on the 'diagram' were the various sidings located on the up and the down sides of the main tracks. These included some sidings which ran behind the box giving access into and out of the Ely Sugar Factory, which was situated just to the east of us, behind the box.

As Jack explained, the main part of the layout, including the nearby entry onto the West Curve - all of which could be seen from the windows of the box - formed a 'five-way' junction. The far end of the 'west curve', where it joined the Peterborough line in the down direction, there formed another 'three-way' junction. This section, Jack told me, had in the past been controlled by a separate signal-box, but was now controlled by our own box. A short way down the line, but out of sight from the box, the Ely-Queen Adelaide public road crossed the Peterborough, the Lynn and the Norwich lines over three separate level-crossings. These gates were all remotely locked or unlocked from the box, so their operation by their respective crossing keepers was controlled by the signal-man in the box.

I learned from Jack that the movement of the trains was carried out under the 'block system', the line being divided up into block sections between the succeeding signal-boxes along a route. The entrances and exits to and from these sections are controlled by the line-side signals. The rules of the system dictate that the signal-man at the departure end of the section on which a train is to travel, has to ask permission from the signal-man ahead before he can send the train forward. It is the responsibility of the latter to ensure that the line is clear before giving permission for a train to enter his section. The system ensures that there is never more than one train on the same running line in a block section at the same time. It took me many weeks for some of the technicalities of railway signalling to lodge in my head, but it was extremely interesting to be acquiring some of the inside information as to how the railways were run.

The communication between the neighbouring signal-boxes was carried out on the 'block telegraph' instruments and the corresponding bells, using coded messages made up of certain numbers and combinations of beats on the bells. These codes covered the descriptions of the various types of trains and also virtually the whole spectrum of the operations involved in the movement of the trains. It was to be my main task to record in the train register all the different messages given and received on the bells, with the exact time of each as shown by the big clock above my desk. The exact time also was to be recorded as each train passed by the box. The register contained separate pages at each opening for UP and DOWN tracks and a separate line in the book was used for each train. The numerous columns were appropriately headed for all the various messages between us and the various neighbouring signal-boxes, from start to finish for each train.

I must say that Jack proved to be very patient as I struggled to understand the bells. When repeating a message received, or sending a message himself, he would slow down his transmission so that I could count the number of beats and get used to their combinations and the pauses between them. Soon my ability improved and, thanks to Jack, I began to truly settle into the job. This, plus the excitement of seeing the main-line trains thundering past the box at such close quarters, meant that by 10pm on the Saturday evening when the week came to an end, I left for home that night feeling that Ely North Junction was a wonderful place to be. I remember, too, the satisfied feeling I had when I handed Mum the One Pound note towards the family expenses out of my first weeks pay, keeping the two shillings and sixpence for myself.

CHAPTER 13

Characters; A 'Real' Signalman; Express on the Wrong Road

The signal-box was operated each day in three eight-hour shifts: 6am 'till 2pm, 2pm 'till 10pm and the night-shift of 10pm 'till 6am. Each of the three signal-men was assisted during his day shifts by one of the two box-boys. The boys did not work any night shifts, which were less busy than during the day, so when on nights the signal-man was on his own. On Sundays two of the men each worked a twelve-hour shift and the third man had the day off; this enabled each to have one Sunday off in every three. The boys worked a six-day week and had every Sunday off.

One consequence of this arrangement was that the boys worked one week with each of the three signal-men in turn. My first week with Jack Haynes had been very enjoyable; he was a happy-go-lucky sort of man, cheerful and friendly and he had done a good job in teaching me the basics of my job. Also, as time went on he was to teach quite a bit more about railway signalling and, joy of joys, allow me to pull the levers! He was a man of about forty years of age and I remember that he was proud of how many times he could 'chin-the-bar' at this age - something he used to do using the metal tie-rods which stretched across the inside of the box. He lived on a small-holding of two or three acres at Little Downham where, he told me, he kept goats and pigs.

The first time I began working with Fred Hallam I was rather apprehensive, remembering my impressions of him when I had first arrived at the box. Fred, aged about fifty, was a short, stocky Lancashire-man with big bushy eyebrows. He was a severe looking man; when you asked him a question about the job, before answering he would incline his head towards you and look at you so quizzically from beneath those big eyebrows, that you would begin to wonder whether you had asked a foolish question. He would make very little conversation and I didn't quite know where I stood with him. But in time I began to realise that his 'bark was worse than his bite' and, as I gradually came to terms with his brusque manner we got on well enough.

One little quirk of Fred's, which seemed quite out of character with the general seriousness of his demeanour, was his habit of competing with our neighbouring signal-man in the box at Ely to see who could ring the fastest on their communication bells. The equipment for sending our messages to Ely was operated by a small tapper switch which you worked by depressing it with a couple of fingers and this could be done quite fast. Having had lots of practice Fred had this down to a fine art and in my opinion he had the edge over the other man. He was able to tap out the codes so fast that an untrained ear would hear them as a torrent of consecutive beats. When you got used to listening you realised that in spite of their speed they were nevertheless punctuated with extremely brief pauses between the groups of beats. Occasionally Fred would do it just too fast for the other man to decipher and he would have to ask for a repeat signal. When this happened you could tell that in his strange phlegmatic way Fred was delighted.

The name of the third signal-man at the junction escapes me, so I will call him Charles. In his mid-fifties, of medium height, rather soft looking and very portly, I would describe Charles as looking rather like Mr. Pickwick of 'Pickwick Papers'. Though he was not as free and easy a chap as Jack my favourite signal-man, he was quite friendly and I got on well with him. When I first saw him pulling levers I thought it very comical and I had to make an effort not to giggle. He would reach forward, very precisely place his signal-man's duster round the lever handle and, inclining slightly to his left, would stiffly lean back-wards as though his feet were hinged at the floor; then bringing the lever back across the frame with him, he would end with a swing to the right beneath the protruding lever, giving the impression that his tummy – which seemed very much in the way – had actually rolled around the lever. When handling some of the heavier levers Charles would have to resort to placing his foot against the label plate of an adjacent lever to achieve a greater pull.

The weeks went by and having got well into my job I was feeling very happy with the experience of my new working life – until one morning, when I was on duty with Jack Haines, something traumatic happened to upset things. During the morning a Lamp-man, a young man of about 20 years old, whom I had met once or twice before, entered the box. His job was to fill the signal lamps with oil and to clean and polish their lenses and reflectors; when he was in our vicinity he made a practice of calling in at the box to chat to the signal-man on duty – and he usually outstayed his welcome. His visits were usually timed to coincide with Jacks turn of duty – I think he would have been given short-thrift if he had tried to engage Fred Hallam in conversation – but Jack, although getting irritated by the Lamp-man's interminable chatter was too polite to cut him short.

The Lamp-man's conversation and the jokes he told were extremely crude to the point of embarrassment, so I used to stand at my train-register desk and try to ignore him. On this particular morning, sensing, I think, how I felt he tried to bring me into the conversation, but I refused to be drawn. He then began to poke fun at me. In spite of Jack asking him to leave me alone he continued with his sport, trying to get me worked up. Having got me thoroughly annoyed at this treatment, in spite of my natural reticence I asked him whether he hadn't wasted enough of our time and told him that it was a pity he hadn't got something better to do. At this his temper flared and before Jack could intervene he came towards me with his fists raised and telling me in no uncertain tones that he was going to teach me a lesson.

The Lamp-man was a big chap of about twice my weight and I was thoroughly alarmed. To try to keep him off as he rushed up to me I instinctively put out a fist – and he walked into it!   It was not a hard blow, but it caught him on the nose and made it bleed. With a look of surprise he put his hand up to his face and, finding blood on his fingers, he really snapped.   Raising his fists again he shouted: "I'll knock your b... head off you little brat!!" Now I really panicked thinking that I was in for a pasting, for I couldn't possibly have stood up to a chap of his size. Fortunately for me Jack came between us at this point and with his patience exhausted said to the Lamp-man: "You ought to be ashamed of yourself – after all, he's only a boy – you had better go!"

Turning on his heel the enraged Lamp-man walked to the door. Before slamming the door he turned and shouted that I hadn't seen the last of him - he would catch me when I left off work and would knock my 'b...block off!!!' Though hugely relieved that Jack had intervened to save me from a hiding, this new threat was something else to worry about. It troubled me for the rest of the shift, in spite of Jack's assurance: "Don't worry about him; by the time you leave off he will have taken himself back up to Ely". When two-o'clock came and I left the box I kept an anxious lookout for signs of the Lamp-man who I imagined might be lying in wait to carry out his threat. I cycled furiously down the side of the track, over the crossing and then up the path to the main road, feeling much relieved that I had seen no sign of him. On reaching Ely I felt reasonably safe and the rest of the ride home was much more relaxed. As things turned out I never saw the Lamp-man again until the following year, up at Ely station, when either he had forgotten the incident, or he didn't recognise me; I'm not sure which.

Feeling like a Real Signal-man

As time progressed my competence increased and I became completely happy with my job, enjoying every minute of it. The early shifts meant getting up far earlier than I had been used to, and a cycle ride to the box before most people were up - 'before the streets were aired' as my grandfather's colourful expression had it. The alternate afternoon shift, of course, involved making the seven-mile journey home late at night. None of this worried me, I took it in my stride - or more literally, I suppose, one would say 'in my turn of the pedals.' It all seemed a part of the adventure of my new working life.

Jack was the signal-man who was the most fun to work with. I was by now feeling quite comfortable with the other two men, but with them I was just the 'boy'. Working with Jack seemed more like a partnership; he gave me much more scope. Often he allowed me the pleasure of actually pulling the levers and taught me their numbers and the sequences of pulling them for the different routes through the junction. Furthermore, whilst I was dealing with the levers he would do my job of filling in the train register, thus reversing our roles for a while, making me feel quite grown-up and responsible.

My favourite time during an afternoon shift with Jack was round about 4.30pm. It was then that he made a habit of sitting down at the little deal table at the end of the box to eat his tea; meanwhile leaving me to work the trains. I much enjoyed this for it was during this time that we used to have three down passenger trains through the junction in quick succession.

On arrival at Ely, the down passenger train from London, Liverpool Street, would be split in two. The first portion was bound for Norwich and the rear one for King's Lynn. Whilst the train was being split the signal-man at Ely station North box would offer the Norwich portion to us on the block telegraph instrument and I would accept it by setting the indicator to line clear. I would then offer the train forward to our neighbouring signal-man on the Norwich line at Shippea Hill. When the train left Ely, the Ely North signal-man would inform us by giving us the train-on-line bell. I would then set the junction points for the Norwich line, pull off the appropriate sequence of stop signals to all-clear, plus the distant signal, and await the passing of the train.

The train would quickly cover the two miles between Ely station and ourselves and would thunder past us on its way to Norwich. As it did so I would give the train-on-line bell to Shippea Hill box, to let the signal-man there know that the train was on its way to him, then check that the train's tail-lamp was in place at the rear of the last coach. The train having passed I would return the signal levers back across the frame to set the signals back to danger and give the Ely signal-man the train-out-of-section bell on the block instrument. The other requirement that had to be attended to, of course, while all this was taking place, was to record in the train register the exact times of the bell signals and the time of the passing of the train.

By this time, the next section of the train was usually ready to leave Ely. There followed, therefore, a similar set of operations as those just described, this time for down the Lynn line; sequence as follows: a). Train 'offered' by Ely North; b). Train accepted by us, and 'line clear' pegged on the block instrument; c). Train offered on to Littleport box to obtain acceptance and line clear; d). Points set for the Lynn line and signals pulled 'off'; e). As train passes our box, 'train on line' bell given ahead to Littleport; f). Visually check that train tail-lamp in place and give Ely North 'train out of section' bell. g). Put up the signals back to danger.

Very soon after these two trains had been through there used to follow another one for the Peterborough line and, by the time Jack had finished eating his tea I would have dealt with all three of them. The feeling of being left in charge of working these main-line trains safely through the junction gave an enormous sense of satisfaction. Knowing Jack, I realised that although he gave the impression of thinking about nothing at all other than eating his meal, he was nevertheless fully aware of everything that was going on and could have instantly intervened if anything looked like going wrong. But I was grateful to him for giving me the chance to have a go on my own - it made a boy feel good to be trusted with the responsibility.

Ely North Junction signal-box in 1989, looking much as it did in LNER days. However, the diesel locomotive, waiting at the UP Main Inner Home signal, shows that the steam era has well and truly gone. The old bracket signal, referred to in the text, used to stand on the same spot as this modern colour-light one. Photograph: Zillah Marsters

Wrong Road

Work went on at the box routinely for some months as normally, that is, as wartime conditions allowed. During the war years the volume of freight carried by the L.N.E.R. increased enormously and the junction was continuously busy. One type of operation during 1942 and '43 whilst I worked at the Junction – and, no doubt up to the end of the war – which upset normal train movement timetables, was the running of troop trains. These had to take precedence over all other trains, including passenger trains. This meant that even passenger trains, as well as goods, would often need to be shunted into sidings to allow the troop trains through. Signal-men were notified in advance, by circulars, of the direction and the approximate times of these special trains so that they could be prepared to deal with them.

There were a few unusual happenings: for instance, I remember an up goods train passing one day with smoke coming from one of the wagon axle boxes; the wagon had a 'hot box' as it was called in railway terminology. Our signal-man - Fred I think it was - had to let the man at Ely box know about the problem so that it could be dealt with when the train arrived at Ely. Another incident, which Jim Hooker told me about, was when an up goods train passed the box without a tail lamp, during one of his shifts. It turned out that the train had actually become divided and I remember Jim saying that in dealing with the situation the signal-men had used some bell codes, which Jim had never heard before.

The most disturbing incident at the junction, in my personal experience, was caused by a combination of two unusual circumstances. The first of these concerned one of our signal posts, which was a tall 'bracket' post, located just a few yards away from the box, at its northern end. Signal – No.19 I remember – at the top of the main post, was our 'up main inner home' controlling entry to the 'up' main line for Ely at this point. The brackets held two other posts, one on each side. The stop signal on the right-hand post – No.21 - controlled the entry of trains onto the 'down' west curve. The left-hand post held two smaller 'calling-on' signals, which controlled entry into the two sidings alongside the 'up' main. One Monday I arrived at the box at the start of a shift, to find that these signals were all out of action, the post having been blown down in a gale over the week-end.

The temporary loss of the signals had been dealt with by stationing a flag-man on the outside veranda, at the north end of the signal-box box, near to which the signal had stood. On instructions from the signal-man, the flag-man would show either a red or a green flag, as appropriate, to up-line trains as they approached from any of the three directions: Peterborough, Lynn or Norwich lines. Train crews operating through the junction had been notified of the missing signal and instructed to look out instead for the flag-man on the box veranda, and to proceed with caution. But, the use of the flag-man had only partially solved the problem caused by the missing signals. His green and red flags (or lights, at night) could take the place of the 'on' and 'off' aspects of the signal-arms, but could do nothing about the 'inter-locking' safety function which had also been lost with the now defunct signals. With the signals out of action, the interlocking of related signals and points was also inoperative.

The second complication on the day in question was the fact that one of the three regular signalmen at the box was off sick with the 'flu. and his place had been taken by a relief-signalman. Now, a relief signal-man, by the very nature of his job had to be able to take over at any one of a number of signal-boxes, over a wide area. To make himself reasonably acquainted with all the different layouts and equipment of all these boxes must have taken some doing! So it was understandable that the man on duty on this particular day could not possibly be as familiar with our seventy-plus levers as was our regular signalmen, who all knew them like the backs of their hands. Added to this, he also had the problem on this occasion of the wrecked signal.

In spite of the circumstances all seemed to be going well and the relief man, who had not visited the junction for some considerable time, was gradually re-familiarising himself with the box. We were busy but, apart from the added complication of having to instruct the flag-man, things appeared to be going relatively normally. The Ely Sugar Beet Factory, located just behind the box to the east, had some sidings and a little shunting engine in the factory yard. Alongside the up Ely line we had two sidings of our own, mainly used for servicing the factory traffic, and I remember a train of wagons taken out of the No.1 siding that day and leaving down the Peterborough line. There were then a number of 'down' truck trains through the junction. Shortly after these an 'up' Peterborough express - bound for Colchester I think - was 'offered' by our colleagues in the Chettisham box. We accepted the express, giving Chettisham 'line clear' on the pegging instrument.

It was from then on that things were to go wrong. We obtained the 'line-clear' from the Ely box in the usual way and all was ready for the express. Normally, as soon as we had received the train-on-line bell from Chettisham we would have pulled off all the signals, including the distant signal, and the express would very soon have stormed through the junction at a fair speed. Now, with our signal out of action, 'up' line trains were having to approach with more caution - a hand held flag could not be seen anywhere near as easily from a distance as could the arm on a signal post. Even so, I remember being rather surprised at how long my signal-man waited before pulling off our home signals for the train, causing it to slow down to quite a crawl before allowing it forward. He instructed the flag-man to give a green flag and the train came over the points off the Peterborough line, just beginning to pick up speed again, as it passed us just below the box.

As usual, I was standing at my tall desk, facing the long windowed side of the box, with the tracks immediately below. Looking to my left, through the far end window at the south end of the box, I watching the train as it moved away from us towards Ely, ready to check its tail-lamp. Our starter signal − No.20 - pulled off to 'all-clear', could be clearly seen in the distance, ahead of the locomotive. As I looked along the line ahead of the train, suddenly I saw something that made me start with horror! Between the locomotive and the pulled off starter signal ahead of it −

were the facing points of the up sidings - set the wrong way!

I could hardly believe what my eyes were telling me. Recovering, I yelled a warning to the signal-man — and it was 'panic stations'. The relief man had forgotten to put the levers back after the earlier sugar train had left the siding - and I too had not noticed the error! The mistake was no longer covered by any safety inter-locking, which normally would have been provided by the now defunct signal and thus the signalman had been allowed to pull off the main-line signals to all-clear, even though the siding points were set for entry into *the sidings!*

There were the two offending levers sticking out across the frame like sore thumbs: the points lever and the locking-bar lever which secured the end of the points. The signal-man dashed to the levers in a desperate attempt to correct the points ahead of the now fast approaching train. The locking-bar lever had to be returned to the back of the frame first, before the points lever itself; quickly releasing the catch he tried to put up the lever - but it was immovable! The locomotive had reached the near-end of the forty-foot long locking bar and, with its wheel flanges now alongside the bar, effectively prevented its movement. We helplessly looked on as the leading bogie wheels hit the points and the engine lurched to the left towards the siding. We stared with bated breath, as there was another violent swing to the right and wondered whether it could possibly stay on the rails.

With great relief we saw that the locomotive was still upright - and still on the track; but it was now smartly heading for the buffer-stops at the far end! Thankfully, as we stood at the window watching the passenger coaches snaking into the siding, there was a marked slowing down of the train, but we still couldn't tell whether we were to witness a crash into the buffers. The suspense seemed age-long!   Fortunately, as we were to learn a little later, the driver had realised what was happening the moment his engine had hit the points and he was almost thrown off his feet. As the engine entered the straight of the siding he had managed to recover, shut off steam and apply the brakes hard. By his awareness and skill he had managed to bring the train to a stand, with very few yards to spare before the buffer-stops.

My reaction to what happened when the train had finally come to a halt – I can only put down to the sudden release of tension – for the scene appeared very comical. All the door windows along the length of the train opened and were filled with bewildered faces, all looking to left and right to discover the reason for the rude jolts which their owners had just experienced. You could imagine them thinking, perhaps: "We know it's wartime, we expect some inconvenience, such as being shunted out of the way of your important troop and ammunition trains, BUT, if you must shunt us, for goodness sake do it with a little less abandon!!"

Before the train was backed out of the siding, I remember the driver and the guard came up into the box and there was a hurried consultation between them and the signal-man. I had no part in their discussions, which took place at the far end of the box beyond my hearing. Strangely enough the whole event never seemed to reach the ears of higher railway authority and I don't think that the signal-man heard any more about the matter. Presumably the trio had agreed, that as no damage had been done, they would not need to broadcast the incident any further. I personally never heard any more about it and, in loyalty to the relief man, for whom I felt great sympathy, I never mentioned it to any of my other colleagues. The following week the regular signal-man who had been off sick was back at work, so the relief man had left us and the situation in the box returned to normality.

CHAPTER 14

On 'Cloud Nine'; Hospital Visit; Future Plans

What with all the passenger trains, special troop trains, tank trains and the massive amount of wartime goods traffic, we were very busy for most of the time. I used to look out for the large khaki-coloured 2-8-0 and 2-10-0 WD (War Department) engines which had been brought into use for freight handling at the time and which attracted me by their smart outline and powerful appearance. Also in use were some American built 2-8-0s which, though powerful looking were very ugly and untidy, I thought, with much of their pipe-work and bits and pieces on the outside.

On one extremely cold and snowy morning the signal-man had stopped a goods train at our down home signals. He was having some sort of trouble – with a set of points freezing up, I think and he sent me up the line to ask the driver to bring the train forward as far as the box so that he could speak to him. Feeling quite excited I set off up the line in the snow. About half-way along, I nearly jumped for joy, for through the snow I could now see the outline of the locomotive and, joy of joys, it was one of the big WDs. On reaching the loco, instead of shouting up to the driver I hauled myself up and into the cab.

The fireman was shovelling coal into the open firebox and the light from the fire made a rosy glow in the cab. The heat from the fire suddenly made me aware of how cold it had been whilst walking along the line. I gave the signal-man's message to the driver, who said: "OK, hold tight" and he opened the regulator to start the massive locomotive with me still aboard – just as I had hoped when I had climbed up into it. I was on 'cloud nine'. I have never forgotten that short foot-plate ride back to the box: the fireman stoking the glowing fire; the sensation of immense power as the steam surged into the pistons and the immense locomotive pulled its heavy train forward. I was as happy as a 'sand-boy' as I climbed down the steps and returned to the signal-box, accompanied by the driver.

It was, I think, the bustling, often hectic, activity of the box which added to the attractiveness of the job – there was never time to become bored and I never felt any reluctance to go to work. Both Jim Hooker and I were conscientious, when on late shift, to make sure that we arrived at the box well early. Then, just as was the signal-men's practice, before leaving for home, the one due to finish his shift had time to brief the other one on such things as the state of traffic, and anything unusual taking place. These matters, really, were more the responsibility of the signal-men than our own, but it was a matter of pride with us to be aware and up-to-date with the current situation. No doubt this was good practice for any box-boy looking forward to the day when he would take over a signal-box himself.

There was one occasion when I was late for work, a very dark morning when I was on early shift. I was halfway along the 'pools' road, as it was known, heading towards Witchford. The light from my bike lamp was not good as the lens was covered by the regulation war-time shield. Suddenly I ran into a big pool of water, about a couple of inches deep, I would guess, which had spread right across the road and into the fields on either side. As I peered ahead I realised that I could not see the road ahead and could not tell how far ahead the water extended. The trouble was - I knew that recently the ditches on either side of the road had been cleaned out and were now very deep. In order to avoid a likely ducking, there was nothing for it but to get back again onto the road behind me. I had to cycle all the way back past our house, and go to Ely by the alternative route via Little Thetford, the quite long detour making me very late for work.

In summer time, cycling the seven mile journey backwards and forwards was quite pleasant. One night during the summer I caught up with a young lady – a girl of about my age – whom I recognised as having seen a number of times before. She was cycling home from her work in a hotel in Ely where, I think, she worked as a maid. We spoke and then continued riding home together, telling each other about our respective jobs on the way. About three-quarters of the way along 'Pools' road, she left me and turned off to the left down a farm track, which led to her home at Grunty Fen Farm. I turned into Wilburton station road a little further on and reached home a few minutes later. After this we used to look out for each other and we cycled home together on a number of other occasions; I became very attracted towards this young lady, but was far too shy to tell her so.

Hospital Visits
In the late July of 1942, after Mum had returned home from her stay in the King's Lynn hospital, Geoff was discharged from his six or seven month's treatment in Holt Sanatorium. Joan, I think, stayed on at Oxford at Uncle Claude and Aunt Dorothy's for most of '42. One year later, in July '43 I had completed my first year's work at Ely North Junction and, as far as the work was concerned, that time had simply flown by. However, Dad, at this time, was still in hospital in Northampton, with no clear indication yet as to how much longer he would have to remain there. He was greatly missed by the whole family.

Visits to see Dad in hospital were not easy, for two reasons: one was cost – for with Dad off work, money was very short; the other reason was the difficulty of war-time travel. On the cost side, I think that Mum was still allowed the three railway 'privilege' tickets which Dad as a railway employee had been entitled to. These meant that the train journey to Northampton would have been free of charge, but even so such things as bus fairs at each end of the journey could not be avoided. We were able to visit Dad far less frequently than we would have liked, but had it not been for the 'privilege' tickets we would have seen him even less than we did.

For the first stage of our journey we would cadge a lift up to Ely in the Guard's brake on our first train of the day through Wilburton, the 'milk' train. Then, using the privilege tickets we would travel from Ely station to Peterborough. After changing trains at Peterborough, the journey would continue on the London Midland & Scottish line (the LMS), via Thrapston and Wellingborough, to Northampton. Wartime conditions meant that travelling was rather an ordeal: trains were often crowded, including the corridors. Many service-men with large kit-bags and haversacks, either going on, or returning from, leave, would crowd the trains and often it was a case of 'standing room only'.

After seeing Dad, our return journeys were usually partly during the hours of darkness, making things even more difficult. Carriage blinds were kept drawn as an air-raid precaution to avoid the interior lights from showing through the windows. Station name-boards had been removed to confuse any enemy spies, and station lighting was kept extremely dim. When the train stopped at a station in the dark it was often difficult to tell where you were, especially if you were not familiar with the station names along the route. You had to rely on hearing the place-names called out by the station porters along the route. On arriving back at Ely during late evening we would catch the last bus back to Wilburton village and then walk the final mile home to 'Station House'.

During one of our visits, Grandad had decided to visit Dad on the same day as us. He travelled from Oxford and Mum and I met up with him on Northampton station. We then all went outside to catch a bus to the hospital. Like the trains, the buses in those days were always crowded and as many standing passengers as possible were squeezed into the gangways. To make as much room as they could the conductors would call out "Pass right down the bus, please". Luckily, we found ourselves at the head of the queue at the bus-stop. When the bus arrived, crammed full of passengers, the conductress called out: "Room for one more only!"

Now Grandad was an impetuous little man. Instead of allowing Mum to get on the bus and himself waiting with me for the next one, he clamped his pipe firmly in his mouth, hooked his walking stick over one arm, grabbed a rail in each hand and hauled himself onto the bus without a moment's thought. Off went the bus with Grandad and we were left to wait for another one. This left Mum fuming, I remember. "Thoughtless old man!" she said, "All he thinks about is himself!" Fortunately, after a wait of about half-an-hour for the next bus, we both managed to get aboard and by the time we arrived at the hospital Mum had calmed down. She managed to avoid saying anything about Grandad's behaviour in front of Dad.

Hospital treatment for tuberculosis was quite severe. It included large doses of fresh air; so much so that big doors all along one side of Dad's ward were kept open continually, both summer and winter, so that the beds inside were virtually exposed to the elements. Dad's problem was tuberculosis of the spine. I didn't fully grasp the reasons for the sort of treatment he was given, which involved lying on his back on a padded, leather covered board. He was strapped down on this so that the only movements he could make were to raise his head and use his arms. How patients in this position got used to the winter cold I just don't know!

As I understood it, the reason for the immobility was to settle fluid in the spine and, at the appropriate time, a piece of bone would be taken from the leg and grafted onto the spine. Dad was kept in this position for virtually the whole of the two years in which he was a patient at the hospital. In spite of doing some reading and some leather-work he learned to do – making such things as ladies purses and men's wallets – life must have seemed extremely tedious at times. However, he tried hard to make the best of the situation and whenever we visited him he appeared quite cheerful and used to joke about life in the hospital, laughing about the snow which he said used to settle on the beds. One of his tales, which in spite of the current food rationing was, I think, rather a 'tall story', was that whenever they had rabbit for dinner he always seemed to be served the head.

On one occasion when I had been with Mum to the hospital, our return journey didn't go quite as planned. The problem was caused by a considerable delay on the railway; the train had stopped as normal at one of the stations, but instead of continuing after the usual few minutes, we were held in the station for about half-an-hour. Then, there was another delay further along the line. We were successful in catching a connection at Peterborough, but on arrival back at Ely were too late for the last bus to Wilburton village. There was no alternative – we would have to walk the five miles home. This prospect didn't worry me, but I felt quite concerned about Mum who was feeling very tired after the day's exertions.

We had left the station and started to walk, when a railway guard who had just finished duty caught us up. He was a man I recognised for he had often worked trains through Wilburton. When he realised who we were, he asked how Dad was getting on in hospital and how we were coping at home. After answering his questions Mum mentioned our current problem of having missed the last bus home. He was a kindly sort of man and was quite concerned; "You can't walk all that way without some refreshment" he said, "You come with me". He led us a little further until we came to a public house. The pub had already closed for the night, but he gave a knock on the door, which was eventually opened to him by the landlady and it was obvious from their greetings that the two knew each other.

The guard explained our situation to the lady and she invited us inside. She had obviously been busy washing the evening's used glasses, but at the Guard's request she poured two small glasses of Guinness, one for Mum and one for himself, plus a soft drink for me. We all sat for a while with the drinks, me listening as the others chatted together. Eventually, feeling refreshed, Mum thanked the landlady for her help and we all left the pub. On reaching the bottom of Back Hill, it was time to part company with the guard, who lived somewhere in the town. Mum thanked him for the thoughtfulness he had shown for us, and he left us for home.

We continued on up the hill, passed my school at the top, Ely Needhams, and then, after turning left we went through the outskirts of the town and soon reached the start of the Witchford road. It was now very late, but the moon was shining and I found the walking quite enjoyable. By this time, however, though Mum would not have admitted it, she was obviously flagging. We were about a mile out of Ely, walking past Paradise Farm I remember, when we heard a car coming from behind. We could barely see its headlights as they were largely covered with the special wartime masks. However, the driver spotted us in the moonlight and stopped to ask if we would like a lift. He was on his way home to Wentworth, which meant that he would have to drop us again in Witchford, about a mile further on.

Mum, ready for a short respite, accepted the lift and we got in the car. However, on hearing how we had missed our last bus, the driver kindly decided to make a short detour for us. On reaching Witchford he turned into Grunty Fen Road, continued along Pools Road and dropped us off at the end of our own Station Road, just over half a mile from home. This was very good of him, in view of petrol rationing restrictions, and Mum was very grateful - the detour meant that she had only had to walk about two of the five or so miles home. One way and another, our visit to Northampton had been quite eventful!

Future Plans

The summer of '43 passed uneventfully, both at home and at work, but by then the Railway Company was becoming anxious to know when Dad was likely to be able to return to work. Dad enquired of his doctors at the hospital and they told him that when he left hospital he would only be able to carry out light work, so it was obvious that he would be unable to resume his job in charge of Wilburton Station. This was a big disappointment: to Dad, who had hoped to be able to take on his old job again, and to us youngsters when we realised that we would have to move out of 'Station House'. Mum, I think, was not so sorry about the prospect of moving; she had never been thrilled about living at Wilburton and the past two years whilst Dad was away had added to her disenchantment.

It was however an anxious time for Mum and it fell to her to look into the possibilities and to consider what would be the best thing to do. Some friends in Cambridge had found an old house there, in Eden Street, which would possibly be available. The house had been empty for quite a time and was very dirty, but the friends offered to have a cleaning session to make it habitable if we decided to move there. Enquiries were made and, after consulting the Railway Company about work in Cambridge, it was agreed that when Dad left hospital we would move to Cambridge.

The L.N.E.R. was very helpful and promised that when Dad was ready for work they would give him a light job as a letter-sorter at Cambridge

Station; they also suggested that when the time came for our move, they would be able to transfer me to a signal-box in Cambridge. To our relief, it seemed that most of our problems were being resolved. It was still not clear just when Dad would be discharged from hospital, though it was indicated that this might possibly be by the end of the year.

CHAPTER 15

A Weird Affair; New Year Joy; Prospect of Pastures New

About the middle of October I was surprised to be told that Ely station was short of porters and that I was to be transferred to the station to undertake a spell of relief portering. I was not very happy about this, but knowing that eventually I was going to have to leave Ely North Junction anyway, I did not complain. Looking back, I have a feeling that it was decided that this would be the least embarrassing way of relieving me of my job at the Junction and replacing me with a new Box-boy there. I was never given the chance to go back to the box; my spell of portering at the station was to last until the time came for our move to Cambridge.

I was very grateful that this period was only to be a temporary one, for I was not very happy as a porter. There seemed to be no provision to teach one the job – you picked it up as you went along. To do the job efficiently it was necessary to be familiar, not only with the train timetables but also to know the whereabouts of all the different stations along the various routes. Having worked at the North Junction I had a reasonable knowledge of the train times and with quite a number of the station names, in the down direction, so could be fairly helpful in answering passengers queries for the down lines.

The up direction was a different matter; there were so many routes and destinations beyond Ely and, as I had never before had any necessity to learn them, it was most embarrassing to be asked for information for any of the up trains. I had never been good at learning by rote and I found that trying to cram my head with all the routes and times by studying timetables was an extremely slow process. Whenever a train arrived with parcels to be transferred into or out of the guards' brake-vans, I was happy: I would be the first on the scene with one of the big platform trolleys to volunteer for the job – anything to keep me from having to answer passengers' enquiries!

The platform staff, of course, didn't have goods traffic to deal with and during the lulls between the arrivals and departures of passenger trains, the porters had the use of a porter's room, located on the Down platform. They would use the room to sit and talk, drink tea and, most of them, to smoke - the latter activity often creating a haze of smoke in the room. The men were a jovial lot and liked to play jokes. There was a small grassy area of ground outside the back door of the room with some plants growing along the side. One of the porters told me that these plants were a special sort of carrot with a marvellous flavour.   I said that they didn't look like carrots, whereupon he dug one up, scraped the soil off and gave it to me to taste. Having never before been familiar with horse-radish plants, as soon as I sunk my teeth into the root I realised that I had been had - which everyone present thought was hilarious.

A Weird Experience

There were some female porters employed on the station during the war; referred to in those days as lady-porters. I don't remember them using the porters' room – possibly they had a separate room of their own. One day a train of empty passenger coaches was stood at the down platform, consisting of old type coaches with separate compartments and no corridor. I was given the job of assisting one of these lady-porters to do a quick tidying job in the compartments of this train. We each had a dustpan, a long-handled soft broom and a rubbish bag. She showed me how to move along the train, open the compartment doors and, reaching in with the broom, pull out the cigarette ends and other debris from between and under the seats, into the dustpan and transfer the contents into the bag. Presumably this very cursory 'lick and a promise' type of procedure was occasioned by the wartime shortage of carriage cleaners, but it certainly was not a very thorough job!

When we had finished this task along the length of the train, my lady colleague told me that there was another job waiting on the up platform and that I was to help her with that one too. So, taking our equipment, we went down the subway to cross the line to the other platform. In the subway we met a soldier, carrying a heavy kit-bag on his shoulder, coming towards us in the opposite direction. He had almost drawn level with us, when I almost jumped out of my skin with shock, for the lady at my side suddenly seemed to go berserk, shouting and screaming at the top of her voice. She stood still and just continued making this horrible noise. The soldier, looking stunned, had stopped in his tracks. I was completely taken aback and just didn't know what to make of the situation.

Fortunately, the station Inspector, who must have been on the platform near the far end of the subway, rushed down to see what all the commotion was about. On seeing him, the lady stopped her shrieking and, pointing to the soldier, she shouted: "He molested me!" Turning to me she said: "You saw him, didn't you!" I was nonplussed – I knew that I had not seen the soldier do anything other than walk along with his kit-bag on his shoulder. Furthermore, in my naiveté, I had not the foggiest idea what she meant by saying that she had been molested. Had something happened which I had not been aware of I wondered?

All I could do was to say that I had not seen the soldier do anything. The Inspector, seeming to understand the situation, signalled to the worried soldier to continue on his way. He, looking much relieved, left the subway. Then, turning to the lady porter, the Inspector suggested that she carry on with her work – which she did without further comment. The lady did not say any more about the matter to me and we completed the next job in silence. I was still at a loss as to what all the fuss had been about in the subway and I was glad when the job was completed and my assistance no longer required. I was also pleased that I was never detailed to work with her again.

Alternative Pronunciation
One of the station porters with whom I had become friendly was a young man of about twenty, named John. He was an entertaining sort of chap - quite a comedian. He amused me greatly one evening when we both happened to be on late shift together. As mentioned station lights were kept very dim and, as all station name boards had been removed, passengers sometimes found it difficult during hours of darkness to know where they were.

Around about nine-o'clock an up passenger train arrived at Ely and John walked along the platform helpfully bawling out the name of the station. Well, hopefully it was helpful, though at the time I was not quite sure, for John, being his usual amusing self, made a slight variation in his pronunciation of the word ELY.   The normal pronunciation, of course, is 'Ee-lee', but John called out ELI - as in the Biblical prophet of that name. What everyone heard therefore was 'EE-LIE'; 'EE-LIE'; 'EE-LIE', as if he was trying to attract the attention of the Old Testament prophet rather than enlighten the passengers. I found it side-splitting, but whether the passengers found John's 'variation' to be 'the spice of life' was, perhaps, another matter.

Final Hospital Visit

We still did not know just when Dad would be able to come home from hospital and Mum had planned for us to make a further visit to Northampton to see him. The date she had decided upon was on a day when I was due to work a late shift so I decided to try to change it. My friend John agreed to help by doing a double shift that day, thus taking care of my shift as well as his own. As things turned out that visit to the hospital was the last one I was to make before Dad returned home.

Mum and I caught the Peterborough train at Ely for the first stage of the journey. As the train pulled out of the station past Ely North box and headed on down the two-mile stretch towards the box at Ely North Junction, I was suddenly hit by a wave of nostalgia and a longing to be back at work at the Junction. During the three or four weeks I had been portering at the station, hardly a day had passed without my wishing that I could go back to what I regarded as my proper job. I kept a lookout on the left side of the train until we passed the junction 'triple distant' bracket signals - the Peterboro' line distant was pulled 'Off' - and then moved to the right-hand side. As the train steamed past the box, I looked up wistfully at the windows and caught a glimpse of a face at a window; probably the new box-boy I thought, looking for the train tail-lamp, as I had done so many times - and I felt sad!

With the Junction now behind us, I started to think about our destination. The thought that very soon I would be seeing Dad again had a cheering effect and, temporarily, I dismissed work from my mind. There was further cheerful news when we arrived at the hospital: Dad had been told that the end of his long stay was in sight; he wouldn't be home before Christmas, unfortunately, but would probably be discharged early in the new-year. After the long spell of treatment lying flat on his back he would have to have some physiotherapy, which would help him to get used to walking and moving again.

Mum was overjoyed at the news that the time of Dad's homecoming was at last within sight and the two of them discussed our move to Cambridge and what needed to be done prior to the great day. We had heard already that the house in Eden Street had been secured and help with its clean-up was underway. It was decided that the rest of the family would be able to move into the house before Christmas; everything should then be ready for Dad's expected return in January of the new-year. After our visit, we left the hospital happy in the knowledge that things seemed to be moving at last - it should not be very much longer before Dad was home again. I was much happier on our return journey than I had been earlier in the day when we had started out from Ely.

Pastures New
My portering job on Ely station continued for a while until the time came for the family to move into Cambridge. The move took place about the end of November '43, so we were able to get settled in before Christmas. I was not very impressed with the old house and the space outside seemed very restrictive after the expanse we had enjoyed at Wilburton. The front garden was tiny and the rear one not very much bigger, certainly not big enough to grow any vegetables! However, the move had solved a problem for us and Mum, I think, was going to be much happier living in the town.

Soon after our move I started work, as arranged, in one of the Cambridge signal boxes. It was the one just below the Mill Road bridge. After my experience of working at Ely North Junction, the Cambridge box was a great disappointment to me. Here, the signalling was electrical and instead of the mechanical levers I had been used to at Ely, the frame held miniature levers with tiny handles about three inches long. To pull these 'off' you simply pulled them forward, on a kind of slide, with the fingertips. The romance of the mechanical levers, many of which had needed a man-sized heavy pull, had gone - quite a let-down, I felt! Not that it was my job, of course, to pull the levers, that was the signal-man's province. But I was extremely disappointed.

The regular Box-boy at the new box was about two or three years older than me. The thing most striking about him was the way he groomed his hair. This was very tidy and carefully combed but very conspicuous owing to the amount of hair-oil he used to keep it in place, the oil standing in tiny globules all over his head. He was quite helpful to me as I learned the new layout of the signal-box and I assumed that he would be moving on to another job and that I would take over from him when he left.

After a couple of weeks I became aware of my mistake: the box-boy was not leaving and there was, in fact, NO current vacancy in the box for me! At the end of my two 'learning' weeks I was, to my disgust, transferred from the signal-box to help in the goods-yard office! No doubt the Railway Company was doing its best for me, but being very disappointed at the lack of a signal-box vacancy, the move to the goods office was the last straw! I complained bitterly about the matter at home, saying that I was going to leave the railway and to do what I had originally wanted on leaving school - to work on a farm. To my surprise, Mum, this time, made no objection, so I gave in my notice and left the railway just before Christmas.

The new-year, 1944, dawned and brought the longed for event that the family had awaited for so long: Dad was discharged from hospital on the 17th of January. Around the same time, I too entered pastures new, starting work for Chivers Farms at Histon, under farm foreman Mr Harry Chambers at Impington Farm. At the time Chivers were still working their farms using heavy horses. Impington Farm was no exception, having a stable of their fine pedigree Percherons and, during the four years I was to be with Chivers, working in the fresh air with these fine animals was to give me a whole new experience. I found that my appreciation of a powerful horse was to rival my enthusiasm for a mighty main-line locomotive - but that's another story...!

———————————————ooOoo———————————————

Acknowledgements

My grateful appreciation and thanks to the following:-

Helen Cross, Zillah Marsters and Ruth, my Wife, for their proof reading of the manuscript and for many helpful suggestions. My apologies to them that after dealing with their corrections I then, unwisely perhaps, added a few more bits and pieces to the text; in consequence, any remaining errors are undoubtedly my own.

'Village Voice' - Haddenham & Wilburton community magazine, for printing my request for contacts from people remembering Wilburton station in the 1940s.

Lois Yarrow and *Barbara Fairchild (nee Lyon),* for their letters in response to the above request. The ensuing correspondence and conversations with them were most enjoyable; it was very helpful to have my memory jogged and a few of the hazier ones confirmed. As Miss Yarrow's father, Mr. James Yarrow, was the stationmaster at Wilburton for many years prior to my father taking over, she was able to describe a picture, of great personal interest to me, of life at the station as it had been in her own youth.

David Young, Editor in Chief, Lynn News, who, in 1996, confirmed my recollections of the old Lynn Advertiser and provided additional historical information relating to the two Lynn newspapers.

Doug. Martin, Area Inspector, British Rail, for kindly arranging a most nostalgic visit to the Ely North Junction signal-box in 1988 and, the following year, a further visit for Zillah and myself for a photo-opportunity. ★

Peter Paye and his book *'The Ely & St. Ives Railway',* for information on the pre-1940 history of the Branch.

Photographs:-
Steve Allen, Photo Editor – 'Joint Line', (J15 Locomotive and Goods Train – p.32.), many thanks for taking the time to respond so helpfully to my quest for a J15 picture, for coming up with a suitable one and for supplying the CD ready for printing.

Len Marsters - Author's late Father, (Wilburton Level-Crossing, taken from the platform – p.51.), a photo greatly cherished by the author over the years for the memories it evokes.

Zillah Marsters ★ (Ely North Junction Signal-box – p.61.), thanks, Zillah, for being photographer, though not a railway enthusiast yourself.

N.B.: All other photographs (pp. 9, 16, 22, 43) – *Author's collection.*

Drawings & Diagrams:-
Thanks to *Geoff Marsters* for Title Page drawing. All other drawings and diagrams - *Author*